# Democratizing the Economics Debate

More than a decade since the global financial crisis, economics does not exhibit signs of significant change. Mainstream economists act on an idealized image of science, which includes the convergence of all perspectives into a single supposed scientific truth. *Democratizing the Economics Debate* shows that this idealized image both provides an inadequate description of what science should be and misrepresents the recent past and current state of economics.

Economics has always been characterized by a plurality of competing perspectives and research paradigms; however, there is evidence of a worrying global involution in the last 40 years. Even as the production of economics publications has exploded, the economics debate is becoming less plural and increasingly hierarchical. Among several causes, the tendency to conformism has been exacerbated in recent years with the use of formal schemes of research quality evaluation. This book documents how such schemes now cover more than half of all economists worldwide and reviews the impact of biased methods of research evaluation on the stunting of levels of pluralism in economics.

The book will be of interest to anyone who worries for the state of the democratic debate. As experts who intervene in the public debate, economists must assure society that they are working in the best possible way, which includes fostering a wide and fair scientific debate. It is this test of social legitimacy that economics currently fails.

**Carlo D'Ippoliti** is Associate Professor of Political Economy at Sapienza University of Rome, Italy, and editor of *PSL Quarterly Review*. He is the author of *Economics and Diversity* (Routledge, 2011) and co-editor of *The Routledge Handbook of Heterodox Economics* (Routledge, 2017)

T0347542

**Young Feltrinelli Prize in the Moral Sciences**
Roberto Antonelli
*President, Class of Moral Sciences, Accademia Nazionale dei Lincei*
Alberto Quadrio Curzio
*President Emeritus, Accademia Nazionale dei Lincei*
Alessandro Roncaglia
*Joint Academic Administrator, Accademia Nazionale dei Lincei*

The Accademia Nazionale dei Lincei, founded in 1603, is one of the oldest academies in the world. Since 2018 it has assigned four "Young Antonio Feltrinelli Prizes" every two years, directed to Italian researchers in the fields of moral sciences and humanities who are less than 40 years old. Each winner is then requested to write a book-length essay on their research and/or the perspectives of research in their field, directed to the general public. The Routledge *Young Feltrinelli Prize in the Moral Sciences* series thus includes high-quality essays by top young researchers, providing thoroughly readable contributions to different research fields. With this initiative, Accademia dei Lincei not only gives a remarkable grant to the winners of the prize in order to support their research activity, but also contributes to the international diffusion of the research of eminent young Italian scholars.

**Business Negotiations and the Law**
The Protection of Weak Professional Parties in Standard Form Contracting
*Carlotta Rinaldo*

**Democratizing the Economics Debate**
Pluralism and Research Evaluation
*Carlo D'Ippoliti*

# Democratizing the Economics Debate

## Pluralism and Research Evaluation

**Carlo D'Ippoliti**

LONDON AND NEW YORK

First published 2020
by Routledge
2 Park Square, Milton Park, Abingdon, Oxon OX14 4RN

and by Routledge
52 Vanderbilt Avenue, New York, NY 10017

*Routledge is an imprint of the Taylor & Francis Group, an informa business*

*British Library Cataloguing-in-Publication Data*
A catalogue record for this book is available from the British Library

*Library of Congress Cataloging-in-Publication Data*
Names: D'Ippoliti, Carlo, author.
Title: Democratizing the economics debate : pluralism and research
 evaluation / Carlo D'Ippoliti.
Description: Milton Park, Abingdon, Oxon ; New York, NY : Routledge,
 2020. | Series: Young Feltrinelli prize in the moral sciences | Includes
 bibliographical references and index.
Identifiers: LCCN 2020000204 (print) | LCCN 2020000205 (ebook) |
 ISBN 9780367342012 (hardback) | ISBN 9780429324451 (ebook)
Subjects: LCSH: Economics—Research.
Classification: LCC HB74.5 .D56 2020 (print) | LCC HB74.5 (ebook) |
 DDC 330.072—dc23
LC record available at https://lccn.loc.gov/2020000204
LC ebook record available at https://lccn.loc.gov/2020000205

ISBN: 978-0-367-34201-2 (hbk)
ISBN: 978-0-367-49231-1 (pbk)
ISBN: 978-0-429-32445-1 (ebk)

Typeset in Times New Roman
by Apex CoVantage, LLC

# Contents

# Introduction

In the Middle Ages, the "principle of authority" was invoked in scientific discussions to argue that something must be true because a saint, a father of the Church, or any other recognized authority stated it so. Today we would not want to accept this sort of argument. Yet I personally believe that two objects of different weights fall at the same speed in a vacuum, or that scuba diving deep underwater for too long can hurt my body, only because somebody (a textbook, my doctor, or mass media) told me so. About everything of which we do not have personal experience, we still today rely on the authority principle. In my view, this is justified. The consequence of our personal ignorance of so many fields of inquiry, and of basic uncertainty about the real world, need not be nihilist relativism. We believe that the laws of thermodynamics explained in a contemporary physics class are more deserving of our attention than the hypotheses of a father of the Church on the same subject because, with respect to the Middle Ages, there is something different in the principle of authority that we rely on today. Not because of the content of any specific scientific theory – today, as in the past, they are always provisional and simplified hypotheses: they are guides for action rather than necessary. Crucially, we choose which "authorities" to rely on, entrusting them with the task of taking all necessary measures to get as close as possible to something we can provisionally accept as true. These authorities are not single individuals but a group of people, or better a whole system, of which the inner working must be such that all others – society, which must trust them without being personally involved in the truth-seeking process – can rely upon their profession.

Philosophers of science have debated the issue for decades, and this is not the place to summarize that literature. From a practitioner's perspective, as a member of the economics profession, I wish to single out one crucial element of the scientific system that makes it a reliable guide for all non-scientists: *openness to debate*. In my view, somebody who does not even understand what some specialists discuss will first and foremost want all members of this select community to be able to fully argue their position to the best of their ability, for all views to be closely scrutinized, and that, when a certain position is found wanting, for it to be readily replaced with one less lacking. Constant, full, and fair debate is a minimum necessary condition for society to place trust in the scientists. And it is this very minimal and crucial test that the scientific system of contemporary economics fails, as I argue in this book.

Single economists take part in selected niches of an overall disconnected debate; these divisions do not result only from specialization and division of labor among economists but also from a division into separate schools that, by and large, do not communicate with each other; and due to a steep hierarchy in the profession, members of a dominant school act as recognized authorities in the old medieval sense, as their arguments never fully face criticisms from other schools.

This situation raises the question as to why society should trust economists. As if it were a small issue, this sums to the more general – political and ethical – question of why a democracy should delegate the debate on the best conduct of economic policy, with immediate consequences on people's livelihood and wellbeing, to a technocratic elite of social scientists. Indeed, it should not: democratic debate on public policy will always have to determine the preferred course of action. Of course, the democratic debate inevitably relies on technical inputs (data, assumptions, cause-effect hypotheses, etc.) that cannot be directly scrutinized by parliaments or governments, but these inputs cannot determine the conclusions of the debate. And because of its role of feeding this debate, a well-functioning economics profession is necessary to both a full democracy and the search for social improvement, and the fact that we are currently far from a well-functioning economics discipline calls for immediate reform.

At this level of generality, it is difficult to articulate detailed reform programs of economics: the profession is a diverse and global one, made up of both academics and highly skilled technicians employed in governments, central banks, and international organizations. As an example, in some countries, universities are centrally financed and coordinated through centralized research evaluation schemes (e.g. France, Australia, the Netherlands, and the United Kingdom), while in the United States, which accounts for an oversized share of the profession, the bulk of the research-intensive universities are not public, and in general their financing is decentralized. So it is difficult to develop a one-size-fits-all recipe even on a single (though possibly crucial) aspect of the profession: that of financing academic research.

But something can be said: in general and at the global level, some ways have to be found to develop a fairer and more comprehensive debate than is currently the case. Unfortunately, recent developments in the institutions and regulations that govern academic research, namely the introduction of formal research evaluation schemes in many countries, appear to be leading in the opposite direction. These schemes should be radically reformed or even suppressed in order to return economics to its proper place within well-functioning democracies. This does not mean that the economists' work should not be evaluated. But its assessment is the proper domain of the scientific debate within economics and not the routine output of some bureaucratic procedure easily captured by the special interests of the people in charge of evaluation.

To clarify this position, the book is organized as follows. The first chapter discusses why pluralism should be a feature of economics and why it is in general society's interest to promote it. Economists perceive providing policy advice as part of their job description. They yield social and political influence thanks to a halo of scientific authority. But the idea of science on which such an image is built is highly debatable. Moreover, economics is a *social* science: objectivity is impossible in this field.[1] That is why it is crucial that it retain a plurality of views and positions.

Although knowledge is always provisional, people who specialize in studying a certain topic acquire significantly more information than the average person. In turn, this informational asymmetry, especially when it regards society and the economy, produces an asymmetry in power: the "expert" emerges as a person whose opinion is, supposedly, more valuable than that of somebody else. This power is reasonable: it is not a hereditary right; it arises because somebody knows more than somebody else (paradoxically, even when they are both wrong). Yet it resides uneasily in a democratic society, with its inherently egalitarian principle. For the individual scientist, this raises issues of ethics and responsibility. For science as a collective undertaking, it raises the issue of accountability. Scientists must assure society that they are working in the best possible way, which includes a wide and open debate and the fair reporting and dissemination of the findings to the rest of society.[2]

The second chapter of the book reviews the recent history of economics and discusses the current state of the economics debate. Simple analyses of RePEc, the largest online repository of economic publications, allow characterizing the previous statement, that economics lacks a wide and fair debate. At least four main trends could be mentioned in this respect: (*i*) a quantitative explosion of the economics literature coupled with a narrowing down in terms of contents; (*ii*) growing specialization of the publications (if not of the authors); (*iii*) polarization between mainstream and heterodox economics; and (*iv*) an invidious hierarchy among and between the two main paradigms, with heterodox economists increasingly less visible and more marginal in the economics literature.

These trends denote a general point: the existence of heterodox and mainstream economics, rather than a single debate, largely depends on the fact that many economists in the past have shrugged their shoulders in the face of unwelcome theories or results, laying the ground for disconnected research fields to grow apart. Today, these unwelcome results are ignored again, ostensibly under the banner of becoming an applied science. But in some countries, France being just an example, the disconnect between different schools of thought is such that there is a real risk that economics will fracture into two distinct disciplines in the future. Insofar as this would be a result (and a symptom) of incommunicability among researchers, it would be a worrying development.

Finally, the third chapter focuses on a specific aspect of the social organization of economics as a scientific profession: research evaluation and its impact on the scientific development of economics. Research evaluation has become increasingly comprehensive, formalized, and widespread around the globe. It is especially interesting because it is a relatively new and understudied trend and because it is a policy variable, and therefore in principle, it can be modified.

Formalized systems of research evaluation are especially crucial, because they affect all economists working in a country in exactly the same way, and therefore they are a force of homologation among economists. Informal systems, too, are increasingly pervasive and uniform, but in principle they could allow for more heterogeneity and local experimentation – whether they do in practice is a different story. In several countries, current practices of research evaluation tend to further narrow the economics debate. While it is legitimate for policymakers to demand that economists justify their claim on the public purse (where economics research is publicly financed), ways must be found for such accountability not to degenerate into a call for conformism.

The chapter concludes with some reflections on whether formalized and comprehensive systems are necessary, and if they are, which principles should govern the methods of evaluation in economics. It will be argued first that evaluations should not be as frequent and on so many outputs that they exacerbate the already serious oversupply of economics research papers, and second, that research evaluation should aim at increasing, not reducing, the competition among research programs. To meet this goal, evaluations should be standardized by research field and orientation, should focus on novelty rather than the elusive "quality" of research, and should allow for different research styles and professional trajectories to develop. All in all, research evaluation should aim at boosting the main goal of economics research, that is, feeding the democratic debate.

The gloomy trends of monism, narrowness, and suppression of pluralism are in no way specific to economics. However, my main point of departure, which will not be discussed further, is that these trends in economics are at least partly responsible for worrying trends in economic policy – and therefore they are especially important due to their direct social consequences. It would be simplistic to argue that the economics debate is the only or even the main cause of such social illnesses as soaring inequality and job precarity or the ecological crisis, or events such as the global financial crisis and the ensuing secular stagnation. But economists certainly had some responsibility, and they have not been simply mistaken. They were looking away, because they worked and still work in an environment where they are rewarded professionally for not even asking *if* these events were possible.

As much as they must justify their claim on the public purse, economists must be accountable for their contribution to public policy choices. The currently narrow and hierarchical economics debate does not allow developing a rationale for radical changes in the course of social and economic policy, for which there is instead growing demand both among students and policymakers, and which at least deserves being honestly discussed. That is why the standards and trends in the economics debate should be a wider social concern.

***

This book was written to contribute to the A. Feltrinelli young scholars prize series, sponsored by the Accademia dei Lincei. I am honored and grateful to the Accademia for being the recipient of the 2018 *Antonio Feltrinelli prize* for the social and political sciences, and I hope the book can embody a beginning of my gratitude.

For comments and criticisms, I wish to thank, without involving them, Carolina Alves, Lynne Chester, Marcella Corsi, Svenja Flechtner, Tae-Hee Jo, Maria Cristina Marcuzzo, Alessandro Roncaglia, Smita Srinivas, Jacopo Temperini, and Giulia Zacchia, as well as Francesco Ungaro, with whom I have discussed several issues discussed here (though he wasn't fully aware of this). Christian Mongeau helped me collect and analyze RePEc data, which is freely available on the net thanks to the time and efforts of a global community of volunteers. Charlene Heinen contributed with precious editing of the first draft of the book. The third chapter in particular draws on research undertaken over the past few years jointly with Marcella Corsi and Giulia Zacchia, as well as discussions and debates with many colleagues who are honestly concerned about the state of economics (I'd like to mention at least Alberto Baccini, Wolfram Elsner, Thomas Ferguson, Jakob Kapeller, the late Fred Lee, Annalisa Rosselli, Antonella Stirati, Francesco Sylos Labini, and many members of Rethinking Economics, EAEPE, and Storep). I hope together we can change it.

## Notes

1 This is not the place to discuss complex issues of epistemology and philosophy of science. Hopefully most readers will be convinced at least that economics must adapt to changes in the subject matter and the economy, and so at the very least economic theory is not an immutable truth, but rather it is always historically contingent (Corsi, 2007).

2 Though both the academic debate and its popularization are important, in this work I am concerned only with the former. In the dissemination of economic ideas more than in scientific debate, the relevance of external pressures and interests simply cannot be overlooked. Yet, in a small volume such as the present one, this enormous topic cannot be adequately dealt with while also considering the intellectual and methodological issues on which I focus. Economists can behave in a professional and ethical manner independently of the sources of funding of their research, or they can be wrong even when acting completely in good faith. Therefore, in principle, it is possible to separate the two topics: the roles of an ethical and professional debate among economists, discussed in this book, and the influence of economic interests in the economics debate, left for future research.

# 1 How economics should be

Economics is important. Let's consider an extreme position. In the *Manifesto of the Communist Party*, Marx and Engels (1848 [1969]) notoriously characterize the State as "a committee for managing the common affairs of the whole bourgeoisie." In radical versions of historical materialism, key economic variables related to the production of goods and services dominate the development of human history, shaping cultural and social institutions on their way. This radical interpretation is probably not Marx and Engels' own idea: as Roncaglia (2005) notes, they acknowledged that ideas and interests shape each other. But such a view is still influential among economists well beyond the small circle of radical and Marxist authors, for example, when a New Institutional Economics (NIE) approach – a "legitimate" mainstream variant of economics – is used to mechanistically trace the emergence of political and cultural institutions from productive technology and/or scarce resources.[1] If material forces mechanically determine social developments, the government would appear to have little room to maneuver. Then one would not see a relevant role for economists qua consultants of the policymakers.

At the other extreme of the spectrum of opinion on the social relevance of economists, we find Keynes' famous quip that

> The ideas of economists and political philosophers, both when they are right and when they are wrong, are more powerful than is commonly understood. Indeed the world is ruled by little else. Practical men, who believe themselves to be quite exempt from any intellectual influence, are usually the slaves of some defunct economist.
>
> (Keynes, 1936, p. 383)

So even if governments were controlled by powerful economic interests, these interests would be understood and pursued in the terms (words, concepts, theories) framed by economists. This position, that ideas are more important than interests, can be found in many authors independent of their political views. It could be traced back at least to Max Weber, and today it characterizes, for example, the trilogy of books by Deirdre McCloskey (2006, 2010, 2016) on the bourgeois ethos as the ultimate cause of industrial development.

I do not think the debate will be settled soon, and anyway both Weber's and Marx and Engels' positions have often been presented in more radical terms than the authors' own theories would warrant. They all acknowledged that ideas and interests shape each other. But to recognize that economics plays an important role in society, it is not necessary to accept this midway position. It is sufficient to admit that in the short term – before interests could eventually bring about what they must, if one is a materialist – the economic discourse informs and profoundly affects the democratic debate on public policy and that it facilitates certain choices while making other choices more difficult. At least on economic policy, it is difficult to argue that economic theory has no impact at all, even though this impact may be indirect and variable across countries and over time (Hirschman and Berman, 2014). That is why Schefold (2018) talks of a "paradox of economic thinking": economists think they can contribute to the good functioning of society by proposing appropriate policies, but at the same time, in their theories, they never consider the prevailing economic thinking as a determinant of a country's economic growth or welfare.

A wider debate on the social role of economists took over after the 2007–2008 Great (or Global) Financial Crisis (GFC), when, from commoners under the banner of "the 99% against the 1%" up to her Majesty the Queen of England, people asked how it was possible that nobody among the experts had seen the crisis coming.[2] Economists themselves accused several colleagues of having created the conditions for the crisis by encouraging financial market deregulation and the ensuing accumulation of global imbalances (e.g. Roncaglia, 2011). Since then, economists have been invested with solving the crisis, acting by preference from technocratic international organizations such as the Bank for International Settlements or the Financial Stability Board and from national agencies such as the central banks, proudly autonomous and "independent" from democratic politics (Dow, 2017).

This centrality of economists in the public debate may depend on several factors: from idiosyncrasies of the political movements that came to dominate politics in the Western world in the past few decades ("neoliberalism") to the definitive consolidation of a recognized profession with its associations and collective identity. Among these elements, especially when one considers the dominance of economics in providing the economic ideas up for discussion, is the scientific authority that economists command.

**Experts wish to project unanimity**

If scientists are to convince the general public of their authority in a certain field, they instinctively feel they must try to appear as unanimous as possible, at least regarding the policy implications of their findings. If all people who have looked into an issue hold a certain position, then most other people will agree it is reasonable to think the same. Doubtless individual scientists aspire to have their ideas sanctioned by unanimity for other reasons, too; if they are in good faith, simply because they think they are right. For the sake of seeing their ideas diffused and hopefully developed by their own followers, scientists can legitimately aspire to accumulate academic power. But consensus is especially dear to economists because this class of (social) scientists has the aim of formulating policy proposals. It is important for them that these proposals appear to be the only reasonable way forward and that those who think otherwise don't just have different opinions: they are unscientific, possibly irrational, in a word, wrong.

Some scientists are very effective at displaying agreement among themselves: physicists, for example, even though in the past few decades there has been a dramatic division (now apparently subdued) among supporters and critics of string theory. After decades of heated debate between supporters and critics of Keynesian theory, economists too have been quite successful at displaying unity since the 1980s. At least until the 2007–2008 GFC, all economists have mistakenly been regarded by the press and society at large as generally supportive of free-market policies and standard-bearers of theories of society based on individualism, selfishness, and belt-tightening for the public sector. Since then, some heavyweights of the profession have become more vocal in their opposition to the status quo of the discipline (e.g. Krugman, 2009; Solow, 2010; Romer, 2016; Rubinstein, 2017), and it seems fair to say that society may have doubts today about the existence or not of agreement among economists.

Such unanimity even within the majority school (from now on, "mainstream" economics) exists only in a very nuanced sense, as discussed in the next chapter. And, indeed, that economics is not a monolith is a simple answer to many wholesale criticisms of the discipline. However, there definitively is a strong consensus on what should be taught to students, especially at the undergraduate level (Mankiw, 2019). Moreover, there is remarkably small variety in the sort of economists who gain visibility and reputation in the public debate. For these and other reasons, in society at large, there is a widespread and misleading perception of near unanimity among economists.

A recent anecdote may be instructive. During the debate on the referendum on the United Kingdom's exit from the European Union, Michael

Gove, then Secretary of State for Justice, stated in a publicly broadcast interview that "the people of this country have had enough of experts from organisations with acronyms saying they know what is best and getting it consistently wrong."[3] In the context of the interviewer's question, he was referring to economists, and explicitly the Bank of England (BoE), the International Monetary Fund (IMF), the Institute for Fiscal Studies (IFS, a London-based think tank), and the trade unions. Right before, he had qualified these acronym-bearing institutions as elitist and in opposition to the interests of the working class.

Similar accusations in the name of the common people against a privileged elite, in this case the economists, were raised after the experience of a "technocratic" care-taker government in Italy led by the academic economist Mario Monti. Other examples could be made. Regardless of the merits of this position, it may indeed be that economists have policy preferences systematically different from those of average citizens (for the US case, this was documented by Sapienza and Zingales, 2013).[4] As seen from the outside, there is something about economics that makes it appear different from the common discourse in the public arena, well beyond the mere use of technical language and methods, including the content of what economists say. For example, Appelbaum (2019) writes:

> In the four decades between 1969 and 2008, economists played a leading role in slashing taxation of the wealthy and in curbing public investment. They supervised the deregulation of major sectors. . . . They lionized big business, defending the concentration of corporate power, even as they demonized trade unions and opposed worker protections like minimum wage laws. Economists even persuaded policymakers to assign a dollar value to human life – around $10 million in 2019 – to assess whether regulations were worthwhile.

This image of a uniform block of economists promoting (neoliberal) policies on the basis of their research and specialist debate is a crucial source of credibility – of authority – for the economics profession. At least, so it had been until the 2007–2008 crisis. Since then, an increasing number of voices have taken on economists – again, taking them as a uniform bloc of mistaken and ideological professionals.

Partly this misconceived view (economists have very different perspectives and methods!) is a fault of our making: a majority of economists try to externally project the image of a cohesive bloc. However, even with reference to the mainstream of the profession, the dominant school in terms of method and worldview (discussed in the next chapter), one cannot say that all economists advocate for the same policies.

Hiding the divisions among economists is not just unfair and undemocratic; it also hinges on a very passé idea of what science and "scientific truth" are. Indeed, there is a peculiar duality in the way economists think of science. When they apply their theoretical models to the study of science or try to empirically investigate research and development activities, economists are quick to assume that science is just another market or industry, populated by rational and self-interested individuals who respond to incentives. As we will see subsequently, plenty of analyses in the economics of science assume all sorts of inefficiencies and "market failures." However, when discussing developments in their own discipline, especially in their practice if not in scientific works, economists are much more likely to describe the history of economics as a story of progress[5] and to assume an idealized scientific debate that necessarily ends in consensus among all reasonable colleagues.

Perhaps this duality is why economists have not come to recognize the responsibility that scientific authority entails.

## Is scientists' authority legitimate?

That consensus among scientists commands social authority is not a new idea: it emerged since science consolidated itself into a profession in modern society, with the associated development of separate disciplines. Already John Stuart Mill argued with August Comte about the consequences of this state of affairs: they struggled between recognizing that expert opinion is valuable and finding ways for this authority to be politically and socially legitimate.

It can be said that throughout his life, Comte's main aim was to understand the place of science in society – including the science of society.[6] He thought that top-down coordination of common feelings is necessary in order to guarantee social cohesion. Even before he thought this coordination would be provided by a "secular religion," Comte (1830) argued that science should be organized and coordinated from above.[7]

John Stuart Mill (1865) devoted a whole book to a discussion of Comte's positivism.[8] He accepted that it "is, in a sense, true" that there is an asymmetry in the knowledge, and therefore in the capacity, to judge rationally between an expert and a layperson. But to the question of whether this should lead to a hierarchy between them, he "refused to give an answer until he knew what use was to be made of it" (*ibid.*). In Mill's view, the proposals for a top-down organization of science carried the risk not just of dirigisme but of true despotism. In stark contrast to the neoliberals, according to Mill, the main threat to liberty in modern society does not come from the constituted political powers but from the invisible and all-pervading power of common opinion. Diversity of views and lifestyles has to be always protected, in society as in scientific debate (Corsi and D'Ippoliti, 2018).

Mill recognized that Comte "does not wish this intellectual dominion to be exercised over an ignorant people" (*ibid.*, p. 303). By proposing a massive expansion of scientific education, Comte thought that the allegiance of the masses to scientific authority would come from those who know something to those who know more. Ultimately, this is still the strategy today. The first sentence of the *Statement of the science academies* at the 2019 G-7 Summit reads: "To reinforce trust in science, we recommend more comprehensive education about the scientific method" (Gaffield *et al.*, 2019, p. 1). Even though three other points are mentioned in the document (better media communication, improvements in science assessment and in scientists' integrity, and better dialogue between scientists and decision-makers), to reinforce the point, the conclusions end in a circle, with the very same argument: "In general, an educational and engagement effort should be made at all levels . . . to foster an informed relationship of trust in science" (*ibid.*, p. 5).

The problem with this approach, for Mill, is that not everybody can be made an expert of everything to the point that the principle of authority will no longer be required in practice:

[t]here is something startling, though, when closely looked into, . . . in the amount of positive knowledge of the most varied kind which [Comte] believes may, by good methods of teaching, be made the common inheritance of all persons . . . : not the mere knowledge of results, . . . but knowledge also of the mode in which those results were attained, and the evidence on which they rest, so far as it can be known and understood by those who do not devote their lives to its study.

(Mill, 1865, p. 302)

Mill wrote at a time when universal basic education was still utopian and a field in which he and other British Classical economists had not foreseen strong public intervention (though he, and earlier Smith, had recommended it in some form). Today, we might be more optimistic and assume that a vast majority of the population could be made to understand the rational foundations of science and the bases on which it relies for its policy proposals.

But the discussion about how much scientific education can really fill the knowledge gap – and therefore the power gap – between scientists and the general populace is probably not about choosing between Comte's optimism and Mill's pessimism but rather a matter of degree. Despite the improvement in general and scientific education since Comte and Mill's times, it is arguably still the case that many people cannot be expected to individually analyze the rational bases of most (or possibly any) specific policy proposals put forward by scientists. Most people cannot avoid delegating these difficult and time-consuming activities to specialists, and they must be content to know that these specialists can be trusted.

In mainstream economic terms, scientific thought presents an agency problem: the principal, society, entrusts the agent, scientists, to do work it cannot or does not wish to do, without being fully able to control what the agent does or how she does it. In these situations, an appropriate contract has to be defined for the principal to trust the agent. Beyond mainstream economics, we could say that an overall social context has to develop, in which the agents, scientists, are induced and actually wish to behave ethically (Dolfsma and Negru, 2019; Roncaglia, 2019).

Luckily, although mistrust is rising on the whole (see the next section), society still trusts its scientists. A survey conducted in the United States in collaboration with the American Association for the Advancement of Science (AAAS, the largest scientific society and publisher of *Science*) found that Americans generally trust scientists, even though a non-negligible share of them question some widely held scientific "truths" such as evolution or global warming. Interestingly, even among those who reject the theory of natural selection and "believe beings were created in the present form," as many as 63% nonetheless think that scientists contribute "a lot" to society (The Pew Research Center for the People & the Press, 2009). Similarly, 67% of those who feel that "science conflicts with [their] personal beliefs" and 64% of those who think there is "no solid evidence Earth is getting warmer" still think that scientists contribute "a lot" to society. Because a majority of the interviewed do not reject natural selection or the notion of global warming, these cases do not represent the average American. Yet the apparent contradiction in their answers shows that many people trust scientists because of scientists' role rather than because they are rationally convinced of the content of what scientists say.

We can interpret this finding by applying the framework proposed by Max Weber ([1919] 2015). He distinguished three possible sources of political leadership: (*i*) charismatic authority, associated with individual qualities of a leader; (*ii*) traditional authority, descending from personal habit and social custom; and (*iii*) rational and legal authority, enshrined in modern law and the state. We can apply the scheme by analogy to argue that Comte's and the scientific academies' ideal is that people would accept scientific authority on the basis of reason, the third kind of authority. However, the results of the Pew Research Center imply that many people trust scientists on the basis of something other than their rational agreement with what scientists say. It could be an individual's perception that scientists are frequently smart, possibly more intelligent than oneself (charismatic authority), or it could be that the historic success of science in improving people's material welfare has trickled down to the scientific profession, giving it a halo of authority by social custom (traditional authority).[9] Either way, science's role in society seems to be not as far from Comte's "secular religion" as Mill and we today would hope.

Economics' place in this context is even more problematic. On the one hand, especially since the crisis, economists fare particularly badly in terms of social trust: according to a survey by YouGov, 82% of Britons in 2017 trusted doctors, 71% trusted scientists in general, and only 25% trusted economists.[10] That was probably a peculiar data point, at a time and in a country when the debate was dominated by a specific topic (Brexit) on which economists had vocally and nearly unanimously opposed the choice that a majority of voters favored. On the other hand, it is fair to say that economics is usually perceived by society, or at least it is treated in the media, as somewhat more rigorous than the other social sciences, though perhaps less scientific than the natural sciences. Economists clearly enjoy a much greater political clout than sociologists or political scientists. What they have not adequately discussed is that with more power comes more responsibility.

In conclusion, the information and power gap between scientists and the general public clearly calls for greater social investment in scientific education, including economics. But it also implies that scientists, and economists among them, must acknowledge their responsibility toward society. Taking responsibility starts with recognizing that science is not a utopic realm of perfect knowledge (economics is even less so) and not every word that a scientist says is an indisputable truth to be passively received by the masses. This should not be surprising: science is done by human beings within a given society.

## Science from the crooked wood of humankind

Even though a majority of the population trusts the scientists, mistrust is clearly rising. In a 2018 survey, the Wellcome Trust interviewed more than 140,000 people in 140 countries:[11] they found that, globally, only 18% of respondents have a "high" level of trust in science; almost as many (14%) have a "low" level of trust, and a further 13% "don't know" (there are, of course, large differences across countries: Gallup, 2019). In several contexts, scientists have been accused of being elitist and biased. Part of the growing mistrust of science – one could mention climate change deniers, the anti-vaccine movement, or the Flat Earth Society – exhibits a frankly illiterate nature, often mounted by opportunistic politicians. However, it would be untrue to represent science as an idyllic island separate from society, in which everything goes well and people are working for the others' benefit only.

The study of science, once the domain of philosophers, has been increasingly investigated by historians and sociologists first, and then by biologists, physicists, and economists too. Formal economic models are increasingly used to analyze the behavior of single scientists, perhaps more readily by philosophers than by economists themselves (Hands, 2001). The results of this interdisciplinary investigation of the science of science have significantly downplayed the realism of the utopian view of science.

For the United States, Mirowski (2011) documents the historical succession of three regimes of science policy. After a period of underdevelopment in the first regime, when Germany defined the frontiers of research, science in the United States took off in the second regime with World War II due to concerns about both warlike technological capabilities (e.g. investment in nuclear research, rocket science, etc.) and operations research (i.e. the study of the best allocation of resources and of the best strategies). During the Cold War, with the second regime of science funding, military concerns continued to shape the level and methods of funding of research and development (R&D) in the United States and elsewhere. With the fall of the Berlin Wall, we entered a third regime of privatized globalization, in which universities increasingly depend on the creation and commercial exploitation of intellectual property (royalties, licenses, and patents) and on tuition fees and private gifts and grants.

There are definite problems and legitimate concerns with the current organization of science as largely a for-profit enterprise that is partly publicly and partly privately financed (Berman, 2012). Both scientists and the public are recurrently concerned with issues such as professional ethics, the diffusion of malpractice, and altogether flawed research.[12] But, for our aims here, the problem is not the degeneration of some marginal phenomena and not even the diffusion of misbehavior that, for the sake of the argument, we shall assume is fairly limited (although, at least in economics, it is not: Necker, 2014). The issue is that society and specifically political economy systematically affect not only the "external" organization and financing of science but also its "internal" debate and the content of its theoretical development.[13]

Based on a political science perspective, we can briefly summarize this literature by distinguishing three sorts of arguments. Political scientists have typically distinguished two kinds of legitimacy of political power (Scharpf, 2003). "Input legitimacy" refers to the selection and promotion of personnel in the political system (e.g. through fair elections) and, more in general, to the idea that decisions are made in a way that involves those being governed ("government by the people"). "Output legitimacy" looks at the performance of a given political system and considers whether the adopted policy solutions effectively address the needs and desires of those being governed ("government for the people"). More recently, Schmidt (2013) introduced a third type of legitimacy: "throughput legitimacy." Her notion focuses on governance and more in general on the political processes that shape how decisions are made.

By considering scientific authority as a source of power in society, we could analyze its input legitimacy by considering how scientists are recruited and promoted and how the scientific sector is organized and financed. In turn, the throughput legitimacy of science concerns the rules and methods of scientific inquiry – the way "knowledge," in the form of scientific results, is created and on the basis of which procedures. Finally, science's output legitimacy arises from the adoption of technology and, more in general, especially for the social sciences, science's ability to improve people's wellbeing.

There are both a "populist" and a more profound way to ask questions of input legitimacy of science. The populist way looks at what is perhaps inevitable: scientists have always been recruited by cooptation. Because only other scientists can fully understand an individual's contribution to (or her skills in) a certain discipline, scientists themselves typically select the new members of their profession, and where this doesn't happen science cannot flourish for long. Thus, studies such as those of Allesina (2011), who tries to infer the prevalence of nepotism by looking at frequent surnames in academia, are not very informative. First, because in practice nepotism is always difficult to measure: for example, people may have the same surname without being relatives (and the frequency with which this happens varies by country, so comparative results are difficult to interpret). Second, because they do not tell us anything about the real scientific merit of those who are hired or promoted in academia (Abramo *et al.*, 2014). But, most importantly, because they frame a social problem in individual terms. It is well known that pupils from disadvantaged families or from poorer areas perform worse at school, and it is not a leap of faith to recognize that the offspring of academics may frequently exhibit an "academic" mindset in terms of critical thought, analytical skills, or property of language. When tackling the issue seriously, the point is how to rebalance the composition of academics in terms of gender, race, or social class and to address any possible direct or indirect discrimination in recruitment and promotion.[14]

But, at the individual level, the guards will have to guard themselves. Besides laying out clear guidelines and enforcement rules, society cannot change the crucial asymmetry in specialized knowledge that makes cooptation in science unavoidable. It may be possible, with time and effort, to overcome the current overrepresentation of rich white men (for economics, see Bayer and Rouse, 2016), but the selection of single individuals into the profession will inevitably be determined by scientists themselves. So science's input legitimacy will always be low.

The assessment of throughput legitimacy is not likely to lead to agreement: it is basically the entire field of study for the philosophers and sociologists of science. Hands (2001) provides a survey of the main recent epistemological debates from an economist's perspective; due to space limitations, I will not attempt to summarize a whole other discipline here but will rather focus on the issues that seem more germane for economics, starting from the question of whether science has changed its nature over time.

At the system level, one can ask whether an oversized focus on patentable research in the life sciences is what ideal free-thought scientists would choose to study. Within the narrower boundaries of economics, one could think of the influence of commissioned research projects in shaping how researchers spend their time. Berman (2012) documents the rise of a "logic of marketplace" in US universities, which partly replaced what she calls the "logic of science" ("the search for truth as having intrinsic value. Science is fundamentally the pursuit of knowledge, in which practical results are an agreeable but secondary benefit," p. 9). She notes that, "as [the] market logic strengthened within the university, it became a more visible and legitimate alternative to the logic of science, coming to exist uneasily with it" (*ibid.*, p. 157).

Similarly, there is a debate on the motives and behavior of individual scientists. Economists typically assume that science could be represented as a tournament in which the main prize is the recognition of priority in discovery (Dasgupta and David, 1994). This creates the incentives for researchers to make their discoveries public as soon as they are reasonably certain about them. In order to speed up the rate of knowledge diffusion, all society should do, then, is to make access to the profession widely available while recognizing a stable and substantially flat remuneration to all those involved. Income should be stable so as not to discourage risk-taking but low in order to maintain the incentive to come first in the competition.

The idea of an open tournament suggests a degree of free competition and level playing field that has possibly never been realistic in the first place. But a more recent concern is what happens in such a scenario when different incentives and constraints are introduced, notably financial ones. Psychological and behavioral research has shown that there can be "motivational crowding out": when instrumental rationality (such as a monetary prize) is introduced to incentivize goals that people were previously aiming for because they were seen as intrinsically worthy; people may stop seeing an intrinsic worth in them (Deci, 1975; Frey, 1997). It is thus legitimate to ask if, at least for a certain number of scientists, the market logic really has or could become the main driver of their investigations and to what extent this may conflict with the disinterested pursuit of truth that is typical of the idealized image of science.[15]

Finally, it is more difficult to analyze the output legitimacy of science. As much as the impressionist painters were fascinated by technological breakthroughs during the Belle Époque, so throughout the twentieth century on both sides of the Iron Curtain it has been common sense that scientific progress was the ultimate source of social improvement. During the Cold War, the prevailing idea was the "linear model." According to this approach, basic research leads to applied research, which in turn leads to the development of new products and/or new production methods. This view has now been superseded by the recognition that basic research is not directly aimed at later applied research and product development, that the various phases overlap and do not necessarily take place in the canonical order, and that ultimately it is difficult to conceptually define and often to empirically distinguish what is basic and what is applied research. However, the main policy implication remains, that expenditure in R&D almost automatically leads to technical progress and thus social welfare. This automatic link is being increasingly questioned.

In economics, modern (neoclassical) growth theory developed from the seminal work by Solow (1956). In this framework, one can decompose GDP growth into a component due to employment growth, a component of "capital" accumulation, and an unexplained residual. It is customary to refer to this residual as the Total Factor Productivity and to associate it, possibly along with some institutional features of the economy, with technology and in particular R&D efforts.[16] On this basis, investments in research are recurrently recommended in order to boost economic growth. However, their real effectiveness has sometimes been questioned. For example, an interesting debate has concerned the impact, or lack thereof, of information and communication technology (the "ICT revolution"): huge investment in the field did not seem to provide a visible boost to growth (Brynjolfsson, 1993; Gordon, 2000). Solow (1987) famously quipped that "you can see the computer age everywhere but in the productivity statistics."

More recently, in her book trilogy on the bourgeoisie, McCloskey (2006, 2010, 2016) argues that "the important flaw in economics . . . is not its mathematical and necessarily mistaken theory of future business cycles, but its materialist and unnecessarily mistaken theory of past growth" (McCloskey, 2010, p. xiii). She agrees that innovations are the source of income growth in the long run, but in her view, the adoption of innovations has historically depended on ethos and rhetoric and happened not "because of mechanically economic factors such as the scale of foreign trade or the level of saving or the amassing of human capital" (*ibid.*, p. 8).

In the aftermath of the GFC, we observe a more radical questioning of the "science leads to growth" equation. Although historians will discuss the ultimate causes of the crisis for decades to come, several economists see it as the last episode of a longer historical chapter. The 25 or more years of "Great Moderation" since the 1980s have come to be reinterpreted as a period of surreptitious stagnation, only camouflaged by short-term, debt-fueled growth. Even with less pessimism with regard to what came before, many authors refer to the period since the crisis as the "secular stagnation." Among the various theories developed to explain this lack of growth, a notable approach takes on a technologically pessimistic stance. Gordon (2016) argues that the sort of innovations that changed everyday life in the nineteenth century and in the first half of the twentieth century have been fully incorporated into US society, and growth from there is no longer available.

> The economic revolution of 1870 to 1970 was unique in human history, unrepeatable because so many of its achievements could happen only once. . . . Advances since 1970 have tended to be channeled into a narrow sphere of human activity having to do with entertainment, communications, and the collection and processing of information. For the rest of what humans care about – food, clothing, shelter, transportation, health, and working conditions both inside and outside the home – progress slowed down after 1970, both qualitatively and quantitatively.
>
> (*ibid.*, pp. 1–2)

Gordon considers the United States the frontier of technical progress and therefore suggests a similarly bleak picture for the rest of Western societies. The most laggard among these could perhaps still enjoy some catching-up, but it would be short-lived. For the case of Italy, Amato and Graziosi (2012) propose a similar idea, with the difference that – as for Japan, Germany, and other countries – one has to place more emphasis on the growth miracle of post-World War II. Amato and Graziosi suggest that this is due to two social developments that again are unique and unrepeatable: urbanization and industrialization. Once done, you cannot urbanize or industrialize twice.

These accounts give clues to a much older tradition of techno-pessimism than that of just the last few years. On the one hand, Gordon (2016) refers to a "clustering" of great inventions in the late nineteenth century: a concept dating back to Joseph Schumpeter. Although inventions concentrate in specific time intervals for scientific and technological reasons, Schumpeter (1942) considered a crucial institutional determinant of technical progress: competitive capitalism. According to him, the rise of the big corporation in the first half of the twentieth century made scientific discovery a routine activity undertaken by salaried employees within the specialized branch of large firms. Both the organization and the incentives to innovate faded away with respect to the previous era of heroic innovators-entrepreneurs baldly financed by risk-prone bankers. That is the reason that Schumpeter expected nothing less than the eventual demise of capitalism itself in favor of socialism.[17]

Interestingly, some economists have reached a techno-pessimist position starting from the opposite premise. As much as the Austrian story favors a large mass of small grassroots innovations, many economists have tended to see the long-run development as the consequence of a few large innovators. For example, in Kaldor's view, innovations are typically associated with manufacturing, which benefits from increasing returns to scale (Rocha, 2018).[18] While not typically associated with it, this view can lead to techno-pessimism in light of the historical process of deindustrialization and the secular growth of the services sector, leading to the so-called Baumol's disease (Baumol and Bowen, 1966). Such a disease (among other things) manifests itself with a slowdown in growth due to supposed intrinsically lower possibilities for productivity growth in the services sector. In this framework, techno-pessimism can also be associated with a negative view of manufacturing itself, arising from its possible negative impact on employment due to mechanization and robotization.

On the whole, a vast majority of economists still think that R&D investments are a main driver of economic growth, and mainstream economists typically add investment in "human capital," mainly implying scientific education. However, there is a minority of economists who increasingly manifest techno-pessimism in one form or another, and giants of the discipline have questioned what we call here the output legitimacy of science. In conclusion, such disparate fields of inquiry as have been summarized here, from history and philosophy to sociology and economics, suggest a nuanced view of science as mundane and fallible, subject to influence from human and social factors. They imply that the halo of superiority that accrues to the utopian view of science is misplaced: to reiterate the point, society must delegate certain specialized activities to the scientific system, but it should not blindly trust scientists to self-organize always and everywhere in the best possible way.

From this perspective, the legitimacy of economics is an interesting special case. Perhaps beyond their failures, economists are blamed for wrong policy choices while politicians claim the merit for good ones. But the effectiveness of mainstream economic science can be seriously questioned in light of recent events. Let us consider in the next section a recent example: the European debate on the most appropriate fiscal policy during and since the euro crisis.

## Economists as human beings

Politicians instinctively know that, if they lower taxes, at the end of the day, their citizens will have more money in their pockets, and if they launch some new expenditure, they may possibly target whose pockets it will be. Either way, if citizens spend at least some of this extra cash, the country's aggregate income will increase by more than the original tax cut or public expenditure (this is, of course, Kahn's income multiplier). Fiscally conservative economists do not usually question this folk theorem but rather point to problems in the long run, because "a country cannot live beyond its means forever." Yet, in the wake of one of the largest fiscal stimulus packages in US history, following the GFC, some economists expressed the idea that increasing the public deficit may actually damage a country's economy and, actually, sometimes lowering it may boost growth. This is the notion of "expansionary austerity" that Alberto Alesina explained to the top European policymakers. He took part in the April 2010 meeting of the economy and finance ministers of the EU (the Economic and Financial Affairs Council, in short Ecofin) in Madrid to explain that "first of all, . . . many even sharp reductions of budget deficits have been accompanied and immediately followed by sustained growth rather than recessions even in the very short run. . . . Second [and here we may assume that the audience was paying attention], governments which have initiated thorough and successful fiscal adjustment policies have not systematically suffered at the polls."[19]

Alesina presented evidence analyzed by Alesina and Ardagna (2010) of historical cases in which OECD countries have significantly reduced their public deficit (corrected for the business cycle) and immediately thereafter experienced growth. Scholarly responses have highlighted that, in the vast majority, these cases were single small countries that reduced their deficits while benefitting from the growth of their trading partners, that at the same time many had seen their currencies depreciate and enjoyed an export boom, and that things are different when a banking crisis is ongoing (Jayadev and Konczal, 2010). The implication of these criticisms is that austerity may work sometimes but not when many large countries that trade among themselves and cannot devalue against each other try to do it all at the same time. In response, Alesina and others abandoned the notion of expansionary austerity and focused on their most pressing objective: they highlighted that austerity is more likely to work (but again, their results have been questioned in the literature) if done by reducing public expenditure rather than increasing taxes.

There is no room to review the subsequent debate: reducing expenditures rather than increasing taxes has implications for the relative size of the public sector in the total economy, and as such is not likely to be an issue that economists will settle on very soon. However, it is notable that the only economist invited at an Ecofin meeting presented his idiosyncratic views as self-evident truths and felt no need to explain the criticisms that this view had attracted, let alone did discuss the applicability of policies followed by small open export-led economies in the case of the single largest (and relatively closed) economic bloc in the world at the time of its worst crisis ever.

Yet austerity is the policy that the EU implemented, partly thanks to other economic works. At a public address at the ILO on April 9, 2013, then EU Commissioner for Economic Affairs Olli Rehn stated that "public debt in Europe is expected to stabilise only . . . at above 90% of GDP. Serious empirical research has shown that at such high levels, public debt acts as a permanent drag on growth."[20] He was referring to an analysis by Reinhart and Rogoff (2010), who analyzed a larger sample of countries over a longer period than did Alesina and Ardagna. Reinhart and Rogoff did not find evidence of a particularly negative impact of public debt except (hence the previous citation) above very high levels of the debt-to-GDP ratio. While trying to replicate their analysis with the original authors' help, Herndon *et al.* (2014) found that the result of a 90% threshold in Reinhart and Rogoff's analysis depended on three crucial aspects. First, they did not just take an average of the countries considered, but rather the countries in the sample were weighted by a certain factor that Herndon *et al.* could not infer – and Reinhart and Rogoff did not explain. Second, Reinhart and Rogoff selectively excluded some years from the analysis, again without mentioning it in their paper or providing a rationale for this omission. And finally, there appear to be "fat finger" coding errors in their calculations (i.e. human mistakes when working on a spreadsheet). When correcting for these errors, Herndon *et al.* found that GDP growth is not dramatically different when public debt exceeds 90% of GDP from when the public debt/GDP ratio is lower, and, unsurprisingly, the relationship between public debt and growth varies by period and country.

There is no need to assume bad faith: the Alesina and then the Reinhart and Rogoff "affairs" show that economists are only human beings and make mistakes, both ethical and scientific. This is one more reason to devise appropriate ways to make them accountable to society at large.

However, perhaps more worrying are the findings by Blanchard and Leigh (2013). They consider the forecasts of GDP by economists working at official institutions on both sides of the Atlantic during the crisis. They find that the more countries reduced their public deficit, the more these economists overshot their growth forecasts. This implies that the official institutions' economic forecasts have not been just "randomly wrong": they have systematically misunderstood that cutting public expenditure during a crisis produces recession. This result, published by the then chief economist of the IMF, casts a shadow on the uses and misuses of economic expertise, and it raises a legitimate concern that economists in the everyday business of their profession may be affected by ideology or other political motives.

To say that economists have political views does not imply that they operate in bad faith or, worse, that they have been "bought" by vested interests. While in several cases this cannot be excluded, in general it is a restrictive and unnecessary assumption. A wide collection of autobiographies (Kregel, 1988, 1992) documents how economists of both progressive and conservative orientations often came to the discipline by chance, pushed by relatives and mentors, or motivated by humble considerations of personal and family sustainment. Once they become members of the profession, they are often motivated as much by an internal logic (in terms of group-thinking and schools, personal career concerns, academic power, etc.) than by a drive to have an external impact on society. The issue is rather one of subject matter: while astronomers deal with stars and planets, economists deal with income and wealth. They are part of the society they study and cannot help having opinions about it.

Moreover, it may be wrong to expect that economics can have the same sort of precision and effectiveness that the hard sciences have. For example, due to radical uncertainty in the real world, Post-Keynesian and other economists have always held that economic forecasts are at best indicative (two famous jokes attributed to J.K. Galbraith have it that "economists give their predictions to a digit after the decimal point to show that they have a sense of humor," and "the only function of economic forecasting is to make astrology look respectable"). Each economic fact is unique and unrepeatable, and there will always be uncertainty and likely disagreement about its interpretation.

It is thus wrong to expect that economists will always be right and, when they aren't, to infer that they must be moved by ulterior motives. Often, they make mistakes because they are real people. However, this definitively shows that more ethics and more accountability are necessary. In the language introduced here, we need to increase both the input and the through-put legitimacy of economics.

A first step in this direction is full respect for other economists' views: recognizing the legitimacy of a debate between competing perspectives and acknowledging it in the public debate and engaging in a scientific conversation that does not exclude or systematically discriminate against certain perspectives. In two words: practicing pluralism. In the next chapter, I will clarify what I mean by different "perspectives" or views. Different schools of thought in economics use different methods and have different visions of what the economy is and how to think about it. This is not a matter of personal idiosyncrasies but of historical traditions that have developed in the history of economic thought.

## How to regain trust

Recognizing that science, and the special science of economics, is not the realm of perfect wisdom does not mean that it should be discarded or that we should find refuge in irrational modes of thought. It simply implies recognizing that scientists are human beings and that, in a world characterized by uncertainty and human ignorance, science is an imperfect tool, with some problems to be fixed to the best of our ability.

Instead, in the main, the response to populist and radical right criticisms of science has been all but convincing. Grassroots science movements have taken to the streets in several countries in the "March for Science" events or, in a more positive way, they have organized initiatives such as "A Pint of Science," in which a leading scholar is invited in a pub to talk about her research in a friendly and approachable way while drinking a pint of beer. These laudable initiatives sometimes have taken the unfortunate basic approach of top-down responses and the G-7, on the assumption that scientists only need to communicate better (Comte's policy).

An example of this approach is a comic strip from *The New Yorker* that has widely circulated in the social media. It shows a flight passenger standing on his seat and claiming: "These smug pilots have lost touch with regular passengers like us. Who thinks I should fly the plane?" He and his enthusiastic fellow passengers immediately raise their hands – predictably heading for disaster. The same blaming of the "regular passenger" can be seen in such newspaper headlines as that of the *Washington Post* of June 24th 2016: "The British are frantically Googling what the E.U. is, hours after voting to leave it" (the Brexit referendum had taken place on June 23rd). The common thread here is that people should trust the scientists because they know better. Critics may have to be understood (hence the flurry of studies on the cultural versus the economic origins of populism), but, ultimately, they are ignorant and should not enter into debates they know nothing about. This is the old authority principle in its most stereotypical medieval fashion.

The parallel between a trained pilot and a scientist is misplaced. To mention just one aspect, it wrongly implies that, as the pilot can be reasonably certain of the engineering behind her operations, so a scientist can be certain of her results. This denies the most obvious reality of the radical uncertainty we face in the world. A scientist may be squarely convinced that she is right, but all accepted scientific theories are only "true" until better ones supersede them. It is not just elitist but actually mistaken to state that society should trust the individual scientists because they are the experts. Society should trust the scientific *system* because – insofar as it is based on open and fair debate – it is the best we have. This is certainly not a new argument, but it is stronger and more timely in economics.

Traditionally, philosophers have invoked respect for open and fair debate on grounds of humility and human fallibility. For example, in the nineteenth century, Mill put forward the following arguments for tolerance and pluralism in scientific discussions (Corsi and D'Ippoliti, 2018): (*i*) that any silenced opinion may be true; (*ii*) that even an error may contain "a portion of truth"; (*iii*) that even if, instead, the received opinion were the whole truth, unless it is contestable and actually contested, those who believe it will not fully understand it and will not grasp the grounds on which it is based; and (*iv*) that all uncontested ideas become sterile and die out, preventing the development of their very doctrine. He metaphorically referred to religion, pointing out that, during the Reformation, Catholic priests were less intimately convinced and knowledgeable of the details of their theology, because in contrast to Protestant pastors, they were not used to debating an opponent and arguing their position. In Mill's view, debate is necessary to provide the stimulus to think rather than passively accept someone else's authority.

Then, during the twentieth century, the traditional approach to the philosophy of science underwent a deep crisis and, as Hands (2001) summarizes, many scholars turned to "naturalized epistemologies"; that is, they started using scientific theories to study science itself: sometimes metaphorically, sometimes very directly. This approach has led to a plurality of methods and results; interestingly, however, most still identify pluralism as a desirable situation.

Adopting a biological analogy (in Hands' terms, with an epistemology naturalized on biology), one could argue that the scientific debate "selects" the best scientific theory. This argument could come in many guises: for example, one could think of scientific theories as if they were phenotypes, that is, the characteristics of the organism (science) that are selected in the evolutionary process.[21] If scientists tend to more frequently accept those theories that are better able to explain observed patterns, then one could be optimistic about the long-run prospects for human knowledge. This conceptualization of evolution, reminiscent of "social Darwinism" or Spencer's approach, is debatable and according to many does not reflect Darwin's own perspective. For example, Thorstein Veblen noted that in society the "unfit," if they hold power, are likely to survive at the expense of the "fit" (Jo, 2019). However, let us accept it for the sake of the argument.

A simplistic interpretation of this argument would have it that, at any time, the dominant scientific view is the best, because it survived when the others didn't. There would be no need to look beyond the dominant theory and certainly no use for incentivizing pluralism. But we should emphasize that this is a very simplistic interpretation. This approach is quite versatile and, depending on which characteristics are assumed to provide a selective advantage, science can be seen as proceeding more or less smoothly. For example, Smaldino and McElreath (2016) show that, if selection is based on high volumes of output (arguably a characteristic of many science systems), then evolution leads to increasingly poor research methods and higher false discovery rates.

But there is a more general point. Simplifying matters, natural selection proceeds in at least two steps: first, there must be constant diversification, in a constant experiment of new ways and new forms of living; only then, in a second step, can there be selection of the fitter characteristics within this diversity. Without diversity first, there is no plurality to *select from* later.

Other naturalized epistemologies have been proposed. One could emphasize the uncertainty of scientific investigations and think in terms of a financial portfolio. As no sane investor would place all her eggs in a single basket, so, collectively, it would be rational to hedge the risk of a theory's failure by having several scientists working on competing hypotheses at the same time. That is, it would be rational for society to always finance several competitive research projects.

This hypothesis has been empirically tested against a strategy of "picking the winners," that is, trying to predict the most promising idea and financing only that, or ex post evaluating the various ideas' success and rewarding the best one(s). The problem with the empirical test is that studies typically measure a theory's success by the number of citations it receives in the scientific literature, a practice that will be discussed and criticized in Chapter 3. But even if we accept this method for the sake of the argument, then it turns out that funding strategies based on financing a large number of small projects are more efficient than funding schemes focused on a few large projects (see Aagaard *et al.*, 2019). These issues will be taken up in the third chapter because they often involve the methods and logic of research evaluation. For the moment, it is sufficient to note that both the financial and the evolutionary approaches to science favor a diversification of scientific efforts.

Another science that could offer the basis for a naturalized epistemology is economics itself, and a popular argument for believing that in a certain field the majority view is right is the idea of the invisible hand in the "marketplace of ideas." Here, the metaphor would be that the theory "bought" by a majority of scientists-consumers (or sometimes by citizens-consumers) must be their preferred one. It is not obvious why it would also be the one closer to the truth, however. Indeed, the majority of studies applying a market model to investigate the scientific process focus on other topics, such as the scientist's individual decision to endorse a certain theory (for example, in terms of game-theoretic reasoning with the aim of maximizing their individual career prospects) or empirical studies on the efficiency of research centers (Hands, 2001). But if, again, for the sake of the argument, we were to accept the market metaphor, we would have to admit that the science market, as any other one, only produces efficient outcomes if and where there is competition. Different theories have to contend in the marketplace of ideas on a level playing field if the "best" theory is to emerge from the game of supply and demand. So we are back to the same requirement of competition as the evolutionist view of science:

> the selection process is not perfect and allows the survival of theories and organisms which are not a perfect fit. . . . If there is a great deal of competition, the organism can survive only if it is very minutely adapted to the environment. . . . But suppose an organism in an environment in which it has . . . few or no competitors. In such a case comparatively little adaptation is required for the organism to survive and it will be correspondingly difficult to think of it as a true . . . theory.
>
> (Munz, 1993, pp. 182, 161)

In sum, regardless of one's preferred metaphor within the science of science, applications of biological, financial, and economic models converge in at least one crucial prescription: recommending tolerance or even promotion of a plurality of competing views. This is also the mainstream position among economists who work on the philosophy and methodology of their discipline (Hands, 2001).

The debate is rather, as Mäki (1997) suggests, about degree: how much plurality should be admitted. For example, Rodrik (2016, p. 199) argues that "pluralism with respect to conclusions is one thing; pluralism with respect to methods is something else. No academic discipline is permissive of approaches that diverge too much from prevailing practices." Depending on which academic discipline he is considering, the last statement could be true.

The game-theoretic, marketplace, natural selection, or portfolio models of science usually consider one of two scenarios: (*i*) a plurality of theoretical or empirical approaches to the same (or nearly the same) research question within an established framework of analysis, for example, competing research labs working on the best cure for a specific illness, or (*ii*) the revolutionary time of transition from one scientific paradigm to another, with a textbook example being the move from geocentrism to heliocentrism in astronomy. Since Kuhn (1962), it is widely accepted that, in periods of "normal science," most or all scientists would work on incremental refinements of the dominant paradigm, without questioning its founding assumptions or established methods. So, most of the time, pluralism can only be interpreted as in point (*i*) previously or, at most, implying that the dominant paradigm must be contestable but not that it is really contested. If economics were like astronomy, Rodrik would be right.

However, it has long been recognized that the Kuhnian interpretation of the scientific debate applies less well to the social sciences (Dow, 2004). Here, the coexistence of competing paradigms is not characteristic of transitory revolutionary phases: it is the norm. And, indeed, the main problem of the practicing economists' objection to pluralism is that it is abstract and totally detached from the reality of economic research. Saying that scientific progress requires wide and fair debate among competing views is not the same as saying that any perspective whatsoever should be accepted just because it is one addition to pluralism (Gräbner and Strunk, 2018). In economics, a plurality of paradigms takes the form of a variety of schools of thought that have emerged in the historical process of economic debates, as discussed in the next chapter. So saying that the economics debate lacks pluralism does not mean that there are difficulties in the discussion of economists qua scientists and laypeople; it means that some economists choose not to seriously discuss with other economists.

Pluralism in economics has a very concrete meaning: not anything goes, but rather different schools have a right to be part of the conversation.

## Notes

1  Thus in the far-from-Marxist *Quarterly Journal of Economics*, Alesina *et al.* (2013) took inspiration from Engels' thesis that the adoption of the plow in agriculture changed gender relations in pre-historic times, to test whether Neolithic agricultural production techniques can straightforwardly explain public opinions on gender roles in the twentieth century.
2  Some actually did: for example, Sylos Labini (2003 [2009]).
3  See an excerpt of the recording at www.youtube.com/watch?v=GGgiGtJk7MA
4  An interesting question is whether their pre-existing preferences attract relatively more selfish and economically liberal people to the study of economics or whether the teaching of economics changes people's minds (Frank *et al.*, 1993).
5  Roncaglia (2005) describes the "cumulative view" of the history of economics, according to which anything relevant that was said in the past is assumed to be fully included in today's theories and what was lost is assumed to be unworthy of further elaboration.
6  In his youth, he was Henri de Saint-Simon's secretary and probably took from him the idea of "spiritual power," suggesting both that science has a fundamental role in industrial society (and therefore it should be publicly supported) and that religion is necessary to social cohesion. Saint-Simon proposed that religion become the application of science and that the enlightened should govern society. Although he publicly distanced himself from his former mentor, Comte later founded a secular "religion of humanity." When founding his religion after

a long intellectual career, a nervous breakdown, and a life-changing encounter with Ms. Clotilde de Vaux, Comte would no longer place science above everything else.

7 "[T]he practice of carrying the questions which more than all others require special knowledge and preparation, before the incompetent tribunal of common opinion, is, he contends, radically irrational, and will and ought to cease. . . . The prolongation of this provisional state, producing an ever-increasing divergence of opinions, is already, according to him, extremely dangerous, since it is only when there is a tolerable unanimity . . . that a real moral control can be established over the self-interest and passions of individuals" (Mill, 1865, p. 302).

8 Mill, who visited Saint-Simon in 1820–1821, was deeply impressed by the early works of Comte. They maintained a correspondence between 1841 and 1846, started by Mill, who congratulated Comte on his *Système de politique positive* (Comte, 1851–1854). Mill eventually ended this correspondence due to their disagreements on the study of human behavior (psychology, which Comte regarded as merely a branch of biology), the "women's question," and different political ideals. Mill (1865) later wrote in his *Autobiography* that Comte's *Système* is "the completest system of spiritual and temporal despotism which ever yet emanated from a human brain, unless possibly that of Ignatius Loyola" (p. 213).

9 This is especially worrying when one considers the dominance of economic interests in the mass communication industry, especially TV and the popular press, and their relevance in giving visibility and reputation to some economists rather than others.

10 Full results are available at https://d25d2506sfb94s.cloudfront.net/cumulus_uploads/document/w5uik0fcsy/InternalResults_170215_TrustExpertise_W.pdf

11 The survey results, as well as the main data, are available at https://wellcome.ac.uk/reports/wellcome-global-monitor/2018

12 For example, reports of situations where researchers found it difficult or impossible to replicate the results of previous research have attracted wide media attention (for the case of economics: Duvendack *et al.*, 2017), or the successful hoax in which three people managed to publish in scientific journals at least three fake articles with no scientific value (Mounk, 2018).

13 Mainstream economists recognize that the criteria and amount of funding affect at least the way research is conducted, the actors who participate, and the pace of discovery (Stephan, 2012). It will be readily recognized that different funding levels may determine different efforts (and possibly rates of discovery) across disciplines – for example, in the United States, physics received a significantly large share of R&D funding during and after World War II, whereas medicine and biology have dominated in the most recent decades (Mirowski and Sent, 2002; Mirowski, 2011).

14 This point is not unrelated to output legitimacy insofar as a different composition of staff may lead to different outcomes. For example, feminist scholars have traditionally denounced the gender bias in technology. A recent application could be algorithmic discrimination, which takes place when computer algorithms systematically target certain minorities (e.g. not showing job ads to migrants or women), ostensibly on the basis of statistical risk factors.

15 The good outcome of a collective enterprise does not necessarily depend on the cooperation or good faith of each, or even any, of the participants. There is a literature on how genuine knowledge can emerge as an unintended byproduct of

the exchanges of self-interested scientists; however, as Hands (2001) notes, the discussion then becomes akin to assuming an "invisible hand" in the "market-place of ideas" (discussed subsequently).

16 This notion has always been problematic: for example, when the residual from regressions of GDP growth on employment and "capital" is negative, this inter-pretation actually implies a technological regress, which nobody is ready to admit. For a summary of the many drawbacks of this approach, see Reati (2001).

17 The Austrian indictment against corporatism and large-scale corporations is echoed today by the accounts of some notable mainstream economists. For example, Edmund Phelps (2013, p. viii) argues that "prosperity on a national scale – mass flourishing – comes from broad involvement of people in the pro-cesses of innovation . . . indigenous innovation down to the grassroots." This process would now be in crisis because "[t]here are calls in America for tra-ditionalist goals long familiar in Europe, like greater social protection, social harmony, and public initiatives in the national interest" (*ibid.*, p. 8).

18 This idea, which we may trace back to at least the eighteenth-century French Physiocrat school with its penchant for large-scale agriculture, has been tre-mendously influential. In development contexts, we may see it behind Lewis' (1954) model of growth, and for "developed" economies, we can see it in many Post-Keynesian growth models (e.g. Sylos Labini, 1984).

19 Alesina's notes may be found at https://scholar.harvard.edu/alesina/publications/fiscal-adjustments-lessons-recent-history

20 See https://europa.eu/rapid/press-release_SPEECH-13-294_en.htm

21 Strictly speaking, natural selection requires various assumptions: for example, the heritability of the characteristics that provide a selective (dis)advantage. It is far from clear that the evolutionary theory of the scientific debate is an appropri-ate metaphor.

# 2   What economics is

Being an economist has only gradually become a profession, and the various countries moved at different speeds. The path to professionalization has varied, too: the first systematic thinkers in economics were often intellectual aristocrats who had the interest and resources to devote themselves to study and debate, or they frequently were the private tutors of bourgeois and aristocrat children; increasingly over time, they were consultants to the sovereign, stock exchange brokers, top-ranking civil servants, or university professors. Their intellectual origins and background varied: from churchmen to practical businessmen, including moral philosophers and crown administrators of foreign colonies. So it is not surprising that until recently, roughly the last 40 years, a plurality of perspectives and approaches have coexisted even within the same country and among people who thought they were doing the same thing (as opposed to today's greater hiatus among the social sciences, for example).

At least in the Western hemisphere, the discussion has always been "global," to the extent that it could be at the time: that is, embracing the Western world. The French Physiocrats criticized mercantilists from many countries, then Adam Smith became famous, on top of his own merits, as a polemist against the Physiocrats themselves; the German Historical School criticized British Classical economists and was criticized by Austrian authors; in turn, the Germans influenced American institutionalists, while, probably due to the influence of Pareto, who taught in Switzerland, the Italians were in a conversation with French economists; and so on.[1] After the first globalization of the Belle Époque, the Western economies and finances were so interdependent that the conversation about macro had to be almost one and, indeed, some saw Keynes' call for the public management of aggregate demand as a justification for the statism and corporatism of European dictatorships of the 1930s.[2] In the interwar period the conversation was "global" also due to the need for political, religious, and racial refugees to flee those totalitarianisms. In the case of economists, they often found employment in the United Kingdom and the United States.

It is during the Cold War that we observe a partial de-globalization of the debate, at least between the two poles of the centralized and the market-based economies. But within the two blocks, we observe either a return of the former refugees to their home countries or, more commonly, a flux of students from there going to study in the United Kingdom or the United States (in the Western block), often invited by their fellow countrymen abroad. When this new generation of students went back to work in the "periphery," they would bring ideas as different as those of Hicks, Schumpeter, or Modigliani. In these countries, one could thus find a variety of traditions: from the cultural heritage of the previous corporatist system to fresh masters and PhDs who had studied abroad (Jo *et al.*, 2018), a situation somewhat analogous with today's China.

Around the 1970s, we reached peak diversity. In the Anglo-Saxon "center," a variety of views and perspectives had increased when thought giants such as von Hayek and Sraffa moved there, and it decreased as successive generations of younger migrants went there to learn rather than to teach. In the periphery, a slow but steady convergence started, toward a near consensus in methods and perspectives. This convergence is what Zacchia (2017) names economists' "homologation." It has sometimes been described as an "Americanization" of academic economics, but this is a misleading accusation: many unorthodox economists from peripheral countries have been trained or educated in the United States (e.g. the Japanese Shigeto Tsuru or the Italian Paolo Sylos Labini) and, conversely, many prestigious centers in the periphery today provide an economic education equal to that of the best US institutions. As argued subsequently, it would be more correct to say that economics worldwide – both in the center and in the periphery – is becoming more narrowly focused on its ideational center, which is monopolized by a few "top" US institutions. I write "top" because that is how these institutions perceive themselves and are often considered by peers and colleagues, but, of course, how to identify the best economic research is far from clear (this is what this whole book is about).

The causes of these developments are an open research question for the history of contemporary economics. It is not possible to provide a full answer yet, but the identification of some factors is possible. To this aim, in the present chapter, I will describe in what sense there has been a tendency to homologation in the recent past, while in the next chapter I will deal with one of its main causes: biased and simplistic research evaluation. To keep the argument manageable, I will focus on trends in economics since the 1980s; that is to say, I consider only the homologation stage after peak diversity in the 1970s.

Benedetto Croce said that all history is contemporary history, in the sense that description and interpretation of the past are inevitably affected by the historian's position in the present. Undoubtedly, contemporary history is even more contemporary, and economists and historians of economic thought are likely to have distinct opinions on the economic events and policies of the past few decades; also, they may have personally contributed to the debate they are to survey. Summarizing recent economics research presents a further peculiar difficulty: it is fair to say that its first characteristic is that in the past few decades, it has literally boomed. It would be impossible to fairly describe all various streams of literature and perspectives on methods, theories, and policy proposals.

To try to overcome this barrier, in this chapter I will take a quantitative approach, using data obtained from RePEc (Repository of Papers in Economics, www.repec.org), the largest online repository of academic works in economics.[3] Being the largest repository and completely free, RePEc probably provides the most complete picture among the several databases of scientific research: we can assume that what is not visible on RePEc – with the relevant exception of printed books, which are underrepresented in the database – is probably not known to economists and can be ignored in a first approximation.[4]

Employing a quantitative analysis allows one to overcome some traditional biases, such as overly focusing on the United States (or one's own country) or devaluing the work of women or other minorities. It does, however, introduce different biases, in particular giving the impression that only what can be counted counts. A quantitative analysis can help identify some questions, but only reading the full texts can provide the answers.

In terms of what can be counted, four main trends emerge as critically shaping economics research in the last 40 years: (*i*) an extension in size and a reduction in variety, (*ii*) the fragmentation of the literature and its specialization, (*iii*) the polarization between a mainstream and a heterodox economics, and (*iv*) a very hierarchical organization.

## Economics has both grown and narrowed

As shown in Figure 2.1, subdividing for simplicity the last 40 years into eight five-year periods, it emerges that until the beginning of the 1980s there were 1,775 economists who had published at least one work indexed in RePEc (from now on, "research-active" or visible economists). They collectively authored slightly more than 9,000 papers, with an average of 200 papers published per year.[5] At the end of the period, the number of research-active economists had multiplied by 11, reaching 21,696, and they had collectively authored 90,620 unique works (that is, excluding the duplication

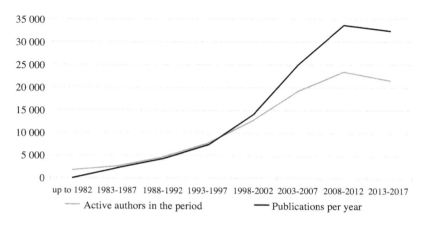

*Figure 2.1* Unique publications and authors in RePEc

of working papers that are published in more than one series or as journal articles too), for an average of 32,500 economic papers per year. This explosion results from both the gigantic increase in authors who have at least one publication in RePEc and by a 60% increase in the economists' average productivity: from 1.55 works per year at the beginning of the 1980s to 2.47 per year at the end of the 2010s.

The sheer size of the corpus of economics research, coupled with the economists' greater writing commitments, have two main implications: economists cannot even begin to read a decent share of the more than 30,000 papers published every year, and historians cannot attempt to know in depth what it is that all, or even most, economists do.

Practicing economists must decide how to prioritize their readings, and by and large they rely on professional conferences and journals (and increasingly websites, mailing lists, and indexing services) to select and highlight what is relevant and worthy. Many claim that the result is an increasing segregation of economists into separate subfields of specialization (Cedrini and Fontana, 2018). However, as described subsequently, this is true only in a more nuanced sense; what we observe instead is the economists' narrow focus on the tip of the iceberg: the research produced in so-called top US economics departments and published in so-called top journals.

In turn, except for studies on single individuals, schools, or theories, historians of thought have reacted to the explosion of economics in two ways (Marcuzzo and Zacchia, 2016). One strategy has been to highlight single features of contemporary economics. Some have analyzed the subdivision of the discipline into formal subfields, often with quantitative analyses of the relative size of the various fields or topics of inquiry (Claveau and

Gingras, 2016), while others have looked at the rise and fall of mathematical models (Dumont Oliveira, 2018) or the "empirical turn" in the discipline (Angrist *et al.*, 2017).

As a matter of fact, the empirical turn thesis – that is, the self-image of an applied social science that has recently perfected its tools of data collection and analysis and has thus lost interest in theoretical intricacies – seems to describe the profession in a way that most practicing economists would subscribe to. But, while economists boast about their newly applied focus, historians debate just how new it really is. For example, in a symposium on "Economics after Neoliberalism," Naidu *et al.* (2019) write:

> Economics is in a state of creative ferment that is often invisible to outsiders . . . economics research has become significantly more applied and empirical since the 1990s. . . . This is important because systematic empirical evidence is a disciplining device against ideological policy prescriptions.[6]

One could compare these statements with Petty's similar claims in the seventeenth century, Malthus' statistical efforts in the nineteenth or the German Historical School's focus on applied empirical work, or Baumol's (2000) claim that the empirical turn was born right after World War I. History, however, does not repeat itself in the same terms: with time, applied work has become, if not newer, at least more respected and even prestigious within the profession (Backhouse and Cherrier, 2017).

The other historiographical strategy has been to focus on specific subfields such as behavioral economics (Heukelom, 2014) or the economics of information (Mirowski and Nik-Khah, 2017). In the latter case, this is sometimes perceived to be so central to the frontier of economics research that its history becomes the story of the main pillar, if not the hegemonic component, of economic thought. Mirowski and Nik-Khah (2017) trace the origin of economists' interest in the concept of information in the debate of the end of the nineteenth century on the theoretical possibility of socialism, which was then reframed by John von Neumann and the Cold War military-funded economics research at the Cowles Commission and the RAND Corporation. According to Mirowski and Nik-Khah, neoclassical economics then developed into three main approaches to the treatment of information, all of which can be traced to variants or stages of Frederic von Hayek's thought.

Even in the face of a bourgeoning economics production, Fine and Milonakis (2009) and Roncaglia (2019) attempt to systematize the contemporary debate in a more comprehensive way. Both document that, in the face of an expanding number of publications, in terms of contents, the literature has expanded from some points of view but shrunk in another sense.

Fine and Milonakis focus on the boundaries of economics in relation to the other social sciences, noting that the growth of the economics literature also reflects a qualitative expansion in terms of contents and fields of application. They depart from Coase (1978), who noticed that

> there are, at present, two tendencies in operation in economics. . . . The first consists of an enlargement of the scope of economists' interests so far as subject matter is concerned. The second is a narrowing of professional interest to more formal, technical, commonly mathematical, analysis. This more formal analysis . . . may say less, or leave much unsaid, about the economic system, but, because of its generality, [it] becomes applicable to all social systems.
>
> (*ibid.*, p. 207)

Coase singles out Becker (1976) and Posner (1977), with their "treatment of man as a rational utility-maximizer," as the originators of this trend.[7] Fine and Milonakis note that this approach, initially regarded with skepticism by many economists (including the public choice thinkers involved in applying it to the "political market") has found greater approval with time.

They distinguish two stages of economics imperialism: in the old stage of public choice and Becker's "economic approach," economists entered the fields of law and sociology, applying equilibrium analysis based on methodological individualism, the assumptions of full rationality and stable and exogenous preferences, and the method of representing all interpersonal and social interactions as if they were contractual exchanges in perfectly competitive markets. The aim of these economists was to test how far the assumption of instrumental rationality could take us, questioning the division that had developed after the ascent of marginalism between economics (based on methodological individualism and rationality) and sociology (based on consideration for collectives and aggregates and on nonrational behavior). In fact, they aimed to bridge this gap by making of all the social sciences a special case or an application of marginalist economic theory, thence the accusation of "economics imperialism."

Fine and Milonakis' second stage of "new(er) economics imperialism" uses similar tools to achieve opposite aims. With the "information revolution" that generalized the notion of market failures to include market inefficiency, incompleteness, and even nonexistence (for example, in Akerlof's "market for lemons" model), second-generation imperialists aim to show how market dynamics are insufficient and/or inefficient and therefore how institutions (however loosely defined) and the "social" emerge as rational individual responses to such market failures. It is still imperialism, but it now aims at integrating some insights from the other social sciences rather than getting rid of them all. Fine and Milonakis thus explain the rise of

New Institutional Economics, New Economic Geography, and myriad other invasions of economists into neighboring fields.

Thus, whereas the folk theory is that economists have progressively investigated more and more topics thanks to a increasingly applied focus and their ability to handle and analyze empirical data (implicitly: to do so better than the other social scientists), Coase and Fine and Milonakis claim that it is the theory – old and new Chicago-style microeconomics – that allowed many of them to colonize various other fields of inquiry.

Finally, Roncaglia (2019) may be the first historian who provides a comprehensive picture of the whole recent economics debate (as mentioned, Fine and Milonakis focus on defining the boundaries of economics). He starts from the premise that fields of research and research orientations (or paradigms) increasingly create divisions among economists and that such fragmentation is the main characteristic of contemporary economics. Because divisions of research orientations and of research fields partially overlap, specialization implies for the single economist a commitment to a specific research paradigm ("methodological monism").

In an earlier work, Roncaglia (2005) proposed interpreting the history of economic thought by relying on the notion of research orientation or paradigm, which he described as the general ("pre-analytic") vision of the working of the economy as a whole. In various forms and with alternate fortunes, two paradigms – one founded on scarcity as a central concern and one focused on reproduction – have always coexisted in the history of economic thought. These paradigms are based on the one hand on visions of the economy epitomized by the medieval fair or the stock exchange, which provided the archetypal representation of the "marketplace approach" based on the notion of scarcity, and on the other hand on visions of the web of connections between town and countryside as the archetypal representation of the "division of labor approach," whose main concern is (re)production. The two visions are naturally associated with a subjective theory of value, based on the notions of individual preferences and constraints, in the former case, and with an objective theory of value, based on the concept of cost or difficulty of production, in the latter case.

Roncaglia (2019) uses this dichotomy to describe post–World War II trends in economics. He reconstructs contemporary economics as the debate on, and legacy of, two key figures active both before and after World War II: Hayek (whom Mirowski and Nik-Khah too have identified as the father of contemporary mainstream economics) and Piero Sraffa. These two paradigms are respectively embodied by contemporary *mainstream economics*, a vision based on the interaction of autonomous individuals who engage in one-off transactions in a smoothly working marketplace (Hayek's legacy), and by *heterodox economics*, based on a vision of the capitalist market system founded on the division of labor and recurrent transactions between sectors of activity rather than between producers and consumers (Sraffa's legacy).[8] For mainstream economics, Roncaglia (2019) describes a "weakening" of the theoretical paradigm due to the progressive incorporation of behavioral insights and the theory of imperfect and incomplete financial markets. For heterodox economics, he distinguishes what he perceives to be the most relevant schools: Post-Keynesianism, Marxism, evolutionary and institutional economics, and the capability approach.

What emerges from Roncaglia's survey is that fragments of the economics literature have grown increasingly self-referential, losing the connection with contemporary developments in other fields. Especially when it is between authors of different paradigmatic orientation, the lack of dialogue sometimes seems intentional. For example, during the Cambridge-Cambridge debate on capital theory, the marginalist (Cambridge, MA) side recognized the theoretical validity of the Sraffian (Cambridge, UK) critique, but it then systematically ignored the critique in its subsequent development. That is why Roncaglia (2019) concludes: "paraphrasing Gramsci, the US marginalist orientation has dominance in today's economic culture, but not hegemony" (p. XVI).

We thus have three possible explanations for the simultaneous growth and narrowing (in terms of contents) of economics, and they are not necessarily mutually incompatible. First, there is the empirical turn thesis, whereby economists have grown uninterested in theoretical disputes and have refined their quantitative methods to be able to approach a wider range of empirical questions. Second, there is the economics imperialism thesis, according to which economists apply their precise but narrow theoretical models to virtually any topic, engaging in "freakonomics." Third, there is the fragmentation thesis that economics can be split up into a mainstream and a heterodox field, where the former embodies a pre-analytic worldview that in general supports the "invisible hand" thesis and the latter embraces the view of a more turbulent and conflicted socioeconomic dynamics. This final interpretation, too, engenders the interpretation of a narrowing of economics, in the sense that the majority of economists become unaware of what is being written by others.

Only by reading the full texts of economics publications can one form a definite opinion on these hypotheses. Probably, each better explains what happened in some periods or for some groups of economists. However, looking for some clues in the RePEc database, we could refer to the publications' "metadata": information such as the outlet of publications, keywords, and the *Journal of Economic Literature* (JEL) codes, which are alphanumeric codes developed by the American Economic Association to form a standardized index of research methods and topics in economics. Considering the first letter of these codes, it is possible to subdivide economics into 20 main research fields (considering more figures of each code would provide finer subdivisions).[9]

As shown in Figure 2.2a, until the 1980s, the average work (that had at least one JEL code) used to exhibit up to three JEL codes denoting two different main fields of research. Since then, the number of different JEL codes per publication decreased to almost one, implying that publications have

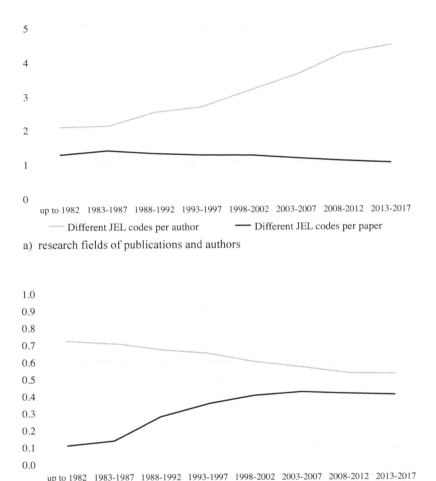

a) research fields of publications and authors

b) indexes of author specialization

*Figure 2.2* Different research fields of single publications and of authors per period

become increasingly focused on just one conventionally defined research field. This simple statistic lends some support to the fragmentation thesis, as each single publication no longer spans different research fields.

But apparently the same cannot be said of the complementary thesis that economists have grown increasingly specialized. Considering five-year intervals,[10] it appears that, since the 1980s, authors have published in an increasing number of different research fields in each time interval. At the end of the 2010s, economists published on average in 4.5 different research fields every five years. This figure is evidently smaller than the 20 main research fields categorized by the JEL codes, but it is surely greater than the image of economists working in just their own narrow field. It would appear that the economic literature becomes increasingly specialized, but economists do not.

Another way of looking at the issue is to consider indexes of author specialization in a research field. Two widely used indexes in industrial economics are the concentration ratio (CR), specified here as the share of each author's most used JEL code over the total number of JEL codes she used, CR(1); and the Herfindahl-Hirschman Index (HHI), which measures how much an author's publications concentrate in just a few JEL codes instead of being scattered across all 20 possible codes (in both cases, higher values of the index denote higher concentration). As shown in Figure 2.2b, we find again a dual picture: authors are increasingly less narrowly focused on just one research field, as evidenced by the decreasing CR(1) over time; at the same time, their publications are increasingly less scattered across all 20 usable JEL codes (the concentration index increases).

A first test of the freakonomics and the empirical turn theses could be based on a separate consideration for authors who specialize in mathematical and quantitative methods (denoted by JEL code C) or in marginalist microeconomic methods (JEL code D). However, I have not reported the corresponding series in Figure 2.2, because they almost perfectly overlap the average ones. For example, the average CR(1) ranges from 71.9% at the beginning of the period to 52.5% at the end, and that excluding authors who specialize in quantitative methods ranges from 70.9% to 52.4%; similarly, the average HHI grows from 0.107 to 0.405, and that excluding the "C" is almost equal: from 0.106 to 0.4. In sum, economists who adopt a "specialize in JEL C + vary applications" (empirical) strategy or a "specialize in JEL D + vary applications" (microeconomic) strategy do not appear to substantially differ from the others.

These results could depend on several causes, and even a more complex quantitative analysis than the present one would always remain indicative only; these hypotheses deserve closer investigation in future research that necessarily will have to imply reading the full texts.[11] Temporarily, though, we can say that the rough and imprecise information that can be obtained from publications' metadata does not seem to lend support to either the empirical turn thesis, that economists are increasingly able to span several topics thanks to their superior quantitative skills, or to the economics imperialism thesis, that they are able thanks to the single-minded application of the same all-purpose individual rationality model.

Finally, it is worth noting that Roncaglia's concept of fragmentation of economics does not simply highlight a division of labor, but it also refers to divisions along lines of paradigmatic research orientation. Within the JEL classification system, heterodox economics is not univocally identified by a specific main research field, but a number of JEL codes at a finer level of aggregation allow for the identification of at least a number of heterodox schools (such as B51 – socialist, Marxist, Sraffian; B52 – historical, evolutionary, institutional, modern monetary theory; and B54 – feminist); moreover, some journals define themselves as heterodox or are widely perceived to be so by the economics community (Lee, 2009). Accordingly, following Corsi *et al.* (2018) in a first approximation, we can identify as "self-defined heterodox" an author who over her lifetime has published at least two publications characterized by a heterodox JEL code and/or published in a journal that is widely recognized as heterodox.[12] Using this criterion, the share of identified heterodox economists worldwide has decreased from 11.1% at the beginning of the 1980s to 8.1% at the end of the 2010s.

As denounced by Roncaglia and many other heterodox scholars, there is a notable decrease. The narrowing of the economics literature does not only concern admissible methods (as denounced e.g. by Akerlof, 2019), privileging quantitative methods over qualitative and historical ones, but it also concerns the diversity of scientific paradigms represented and cultivated within the discipline, which is quickly converging to a single-paradigm science.

The interpretation of the current economics debate in terms of a bipartition between mainstream and heterodox economics corresponds to the (self-) perception of many economists who identify as doing something different from much of the discipline. However, it is a contested interpretation, and, in any case, the identification and definition of precisely what is mainstream and what is heterodox are not yet agreed upon. They will be the subject of the next two sections.

## Is there a mainstream and a heterodox economics?

The debate on whether it is scientifically legitimate for economics to be split between competing research paradigms – that is, whether heterodox economists have citizenship rights in the profession – has led to the more existential debate around whether a heterodox economics exists at all or if holdouts of a "dying out sect" (Tabellini, 2006, p. 32) are not instead wasting public resources and everybody's time. For example, according to Cahuc and Zylberberg (2016), economic science produces knowledge to treat social ills just like medicine does for human illnesses; economists surely disagree on many points, but when there is consensus among those who publish in the top journals, then that consensus should be considered the scientific truth about it, and those who deny it are akin to negationists (the far-right deniers of the historical reality of the holocaust).

Criticism, however, also comes from within. Some economists who are not identified as developing the same theories that most others do, such as Deirdre McCloskey, David Colander, or Jan Kregel, object to the label of "heterodox," and many others do on tactical or strategic grounds. Some heterodox schools consider other heterodox approaches "special cases" of their own, or they consider them simply wrong (D'Ippoliti and Roncaglia, 2015). Bibliometric evidence suggests that up to very recently, many heterodox schools have not typically engaged with each other, but rather they have focused on criticizing the mainstream (Dobusch and Kapeller, 2012).

There is, if not criticism, at least widespread confusion. Wrenn (2007) interviewed eight historians of economic thought, asking their opinions of the relative place of heterodox and mainstream economics; she found that:

> two professors were not interested in describing the boundary between the two camps. One professor described the boundary as a continuum, one as a threshold, and one as an overlapping area. . . . Two professors stated that the boundary consisted over a continuum with an overlapping area. The final professor suggested that the boundary consisted of a threshold and a continuum.

Such confusion and incoherence lead Hodgson (2019) to say that the field is only bound together by the common opposition to capitalism. But these criticisms may be increasingly outdated. Especially since the global financial crisis, things are changing. On the one hand, more cohesion and coherence among the heterodox schools are emerging thanks to the purposeful establishment of professional and social institutions such as "big tent" conferences, pluralist journals, and joint dissemination efforts such as websites, newsletters, and so on (Lee, 2009). On the other hand, an increasing number of economists embrace a scientific commitment to valuing pluralism. Proponents affirm that a plurality of methods and perspectives is necessary to understand complex real-world phenomena; schools of thought focus on understanding reality differently or throwing light on different aspects of reality, and their integration is thus a form of complementarity (Dow, 2004).

Possible definitions of heterodox economics that aim at highlighting its internal coherence have been put forward, for example, by Lee (2009)[13] and Jo *et al.* (2018), according to whom heterodox economics is an alliance of several schools and traditions of economic research that propose an analysis of social provisioning "focusing on a wide range of economic and social activities in a socio-historical context, including both market and non-market, paid and unpaid activities, undertaken by human beings and going-concerns to ensure their survival and reproduction" (Jo *et al.*, 2018, p. 10). But this sort of definition is very vague and does not precisely draw a boundary between heterodox and mainstream economics.[14] That is why many heterodox economists (including Fred Lee himself) rather refer to the marginalist theory of prices, as determined by the market clearing condition of supply and demand, as the main feature of mainstream economics and therefore its rejection as the identifying characteristic of heterodox economics (D'Ippoliti and Roncaglia, 2015).

Let us accept for the moment this narrower definition, to highlight that the hunt for the perfect definition misses the main point. Within heterodox economics, plurality descends from the historical development of economic thought in different countries and within separate but connected communities. It encompasses at least Sraffian and Post-Keynesian economics, feminist economics, ecological economics, Marxian and radical economics, the *régulation* approach, (old) institutional economics, evolutionary economics, possibly part of Austrian economics, and others – all because these schools have historically developed after the seminal contributions of key figures of the past, whose work heterodox economists still consider relevant today.

Truly, some aspects of theories of the past can be considered wrong. Ricardo was aware that his labor theory of value was logically defective, and throughout his life he worked on trying to fix it; today, Shaikh (2016) employs an empirical approach to try to salvage Marx's labor theory of value, but no one can legitimately deny the "truth" that its mathematical logic requires at least a reformulation.

However, other theories of the founders or inspirers of current heterodox approaches have not been disproved so far: for example, earlier, I referred to the Cambridge debate on capital theory. More than 50 years after that debate, the (very) few mainstream economists who are still interested in the theoretical foundations of their models must conclude that the neoclassical aggregate production function (implying that the rate of interest is determined by technology and that the distribution of income is determined by the relative scarcity of labor and "capital" – in sum, the core of mainstream economics) "does not work outside of very special cases" (Baqaee and Fahri, 2019, p. 1362). Yet, for the most part, mainstream economists continue to develop models based on aggregate production functions or to assume that wages depend on workers' marginal productivity.

Other examples could be made. Keynes, in his *Treatise on Probability*, argued that probability theory is a branch of logic: "once the facts are given which determine our knowledge, what is probable or improbable . . . has been fixed objectively, and is independent of our opinion" (Keynes, 1921, p. 3). However, most of the time, "the facts" are not "given," in the sense that we do not have full information about them. Actually, cases of complete information or complete ignorance are extreme, and according to Keynes, most economic decisions are taken in intermediate situations, of which we know something but not everything (and we know we don't). In those cases, behavior cannot be objectively rational, because it is not clear at all what would be rational to do when we don't have full knowledge of the situation.[15] This point is accepted by many mainstream economists: for example, Knight famously distinguished between "risk" (when we know the possible scenarios and can assign probabilities to them) and "uncertainty" (when we don't fully know). However, with very few exceptions (e.g. within behavioral economics) the mainstream response has been to simply assume risk conditions only and rational behavior as a rule. By contrast, Post-Keynesians have focused on what happens to investment, money, and finance when people must decide what to do without knowing what is objectively probable or improbable. Investment and financial decisions are especially interesting in this light, because they concern the future, of which we necessarily know less than the present. Even if one disagrees with Keynes and thinks that a majority of economic decisions are taken in situations of which we know everything (cases of risk, in Knight's terminology), it is difficult to see how the sort of situations studied by the Post-Keynesians are not relevant at least in some cases or at certain times. Thus, they should retain a legitimate place within economics.

Further examples of the historical roots of current heterodox approaches could be made. The point here is that these theories must retain citizenship in the citadel of economics, at least until their opposers make the effort of convincingly criticizing them. That is why it is vulgar to assume that pluralism – respect for the coexistence of different research paradigms – implies an "anything goes" attitude. It is not about letting the barbarians in at the gate but having the intellectual honesty of distinguishing between theories of the past that have been disproved and theories that have not.

The existence of heterodox and mainstream economics largely depends on the fact that many colleagues in the past have simply shrugged their shoulders in the face of unwelcome theories or results, laying the ground for disconnected research fields to grow apart.

## Why mainstream pluralism is not enough

If heterodox economics is characterized by plurality, to some extent, mainstream economics exhibits internal diversity, too. That is why some reject the notion of "mainstream economics" as a coherent whole (Colander *et al.*, 2004), and others talk of a "mainstream pluralism" (Davis, 2006). With time, different fields such as evolutionary game theory, behavioral and experimental economics, neuroeconomics, or New Institutional Economics have developed idiosyncratic hypotheses, and typically they have come to rely on methods and assumptions common only in their domain of specialty. Crucially, these subfields recurrently produce contrasting results among themselves, so that one can never really claim that "mainstream economics assumes this" or "mainstream economics claims that." You will always find a stream of mainstream economics that does not. So it is not rare for macro models to assume forward-looking infinite-living agents who are selfish, perfectly rational, and fully informed; nor would it be strange for a behavioral economist to assume exactly the contrary: myopia, limited information, bounded rationality, and even solidarity or altruism.[16]

The result is what Kapeller (2013) calls "axiomatic variation": whereas natural scientists typically vary the auxiliary hypotheses they use in order to apply a set of general laws to explain a new fact or a specific phenomenon, mainstream economists have come to accept that any assumption may be changed, even if it is an explanatory assumption in a given context, that is, even if it should be considered a general law that characterizes the whole scientific paradigm. Because of axiomatic variation, it has become difficult to coherently define mainstream economics and, therefore, to identify what lies outside of it. Some authors focus on formal elements of single theoretical models; Lawson (2003) singles out the use of mathematics because in his view, it is inappropriate to an "open system" such as human society; Roncaglia (2019), as noted previously, points to the conceptual compatibility with a certain pre-analytical vision of the economic system as a whole.

Perhaps part of the disagreement arises because different authors use the terms "neoclassical," "marginalist," and "mainstream" in different (sometimes interchangeable) ways. Although it was implicit, in this work I use "mainstream economics" to simply denote what the majority of economists ("mainstream economists") do. It is a descriptive term that pertains to the sociology of the profession, but it is not devoid of theoretical content. There must be a certain glue within the mainstream, both in terms of theory and of the economists' self-identity; otherwise, we would be talking about different disciplines. The question thus stands: what theory do the majority of economists share?

An appropriate answer may be based on Eco (1995). The Italian philosopher answered those who tried to downplay Mussolini's responsibilities, as compared to Hitler's, by noting that "Fascism was a *fuzzy* totalitarianism, a collage of different philosophical and political ideas, a beehive of contradictions." But despite this incoherence, especially when comparing totalitarianisms across countries, one can recognize some common archetypal traits. Eco recalls Wittgenstein's notion of a "game," that is, a collection of disparate activities that yet display some "family resemblance." Consider the following sequence:

| 1 | 2 | 3 | 4 |
|---|---|---|---|
| abc | bcd | cde | def |

Contiguous elements share two letters; elements 1 and 3 have "c" in common, and 2 and 4 have "d" in common. However, elements 1 and 4 do not have anything in common. Yet, Eco notices, "owing to the uninterrupted series of decreasing similarities between one and four, there remains, by a sort of illusory transitivity, a family resemblance between four and one."

Mainstream economics is in a similar situation: with respect to a well-defined *core* of tenets, each subfield of the mainstream typically refers to only a part of it. Contiguous fields share more than they do with the others, and some fields share very little indeed. The core, however, is the common benchmark that gives the family resemblance to all. An explanatory and non-exhaustive list of elements that characterize such a core could be the following:

- concerning ontology, the assumption that the social world is closed and divisible; that is, it can always be analyzed by separating out elements to be included in a formal, often mathematical, model, which may allow for calculable risk but not for uncertainty;
- concerning method, the assumptions that social phenomena are best understood starting from the individual (methodological individualism) and that aggregate phenomena are the sum of individual components;
- concerning theory, the assumptions that: there is an exogenously given scarcity of resources, and it is binding (i.e. human wants are always greater than the available resources are able to satisfy); people are different for exogenous reasons (heterogeneity); they have given and stable preferences, and these are the only rationale of agency; they are informed and rational and make decisions on the basis of cost-benefit analysis (utility maximization or cost minimization); choice is the only cause of behavior; all interpersonal interactions can be seen as contracts bargained in competitive markets; and in all (really existing or supposed) markets, equilibrium prices are determined by the equality of the quantities demanded and supplied, and no exchange takes place outside of this equilibrium.

These elements are virtually never all simultaneously present. However, for mainstream economists, they represent the archetypal notion of what economics is, even though "at the frontier of research," they take the liberty of innovating by changing an increasing number of features simultaneously. What Akerlof (2019) calls "one-deviation-at-a-timism" is dying: now two or three deviations at a time may be acceptable, the core is not changing or losing its role as a benchmark. That is why, truly, there is some internal plurality within the mainstream, but this is not enough for us to say that economics is already pluralist, without the need for heterodox economics. Heterodox economists do not just avoid, they criticize and oppose (almost) all the previous elements of the core, and they depart from an alternative list of – frequently opposite – axioms.

Moreover, even if there is some theoretical flexibility within economics research, mainstream economists are not allowed the same latitude when it comes to teaching. Especially at the undergraduate level, it is assumed that students must know the core of the discipline and just that. Only in more advanced stages of their studies, if at all, may they be allowed to become familiar with more critical attitudes or alternative approaches.

For example, Mankiw (2019), the author of possibly the most popular macro textbooks in the world, writes:

> Just as ambassadors are supposed to faithfully represent the perspective of their nations, the instructor in an introductory course (and intermediate courses as well) should faithfully represent the views shared by *the majority* of professional economists. . . . This perspective of instructor as ambassador raises the question of what instructors should do if they hold views far from the mainstream of the economics profession. If you are an Austrian or Marxist economist, for example, what should you do if asked to teach an introductory course? In my view, there are only two responsible courses of action. One is to sublimate your own views and spend most of the course teaching what the mainstream believes, even if you disagree with it. . . . The other responsible course of action is to avoid teaching introductory (and even intermediate) courses entirely.
>
> (pp. 2–4, my emphasis)

Incidentally, it is worth recalling that, according to article 3 of the 1961 Vienna Convention on Diplomatic Relations, diplomatic missions "represent the sending *State*," and they can negotiate "with the *Government* of the receiving State" (my emphasis). Since we never have unanimity of views (both within a State and within economics), Mankiw's confusion of the state, which encompasses all citizens, with the government, which is an expression of the pro-tempore ruling majority, exemplifies the anti-democratic bias in his position, which basically ignores the minority.

I discussed in the previous chapter the reasons one does not wish to see a mono-thinking within economics research, but the issue is wider when dealing with economics teaching. Many who study using Mankiw's textbooks will not go on to study economics at a higher level: they may choose journalism, law, political science, or sociology instead. Therefore, the approach of teaching only mainstream economics at the undergraduate level and maybe postponing (if teaching at all) criticisms and alternatives until later specialized courses has two main consequences: (*i*) it reinforces among the non-economists the idea that the previously described core is the "truth" in economics, and (*ii*) it gives economics students the idea that the core is the set of important basic principles to be known and remembered, while criticisms and alternatives are an interesting curiosum for those who specialize in a certain subfield.

To the extent that "principles of economics" courses actually mean "introduction to mainstream economics only," it is no surprise that scholars of other disciplines as well as journalists and the general public think that economics is mainstream economics, and they have never heard of heterodox economics. This restricts the political and democratic debate, although not, as sometimes it is claimed, in the superficial sense that economists are all banner-bearers of free-market policies and the moneyed interests.

## Is mainstream economics "neoliberal"?

In opposition to conservative thinking that assumed a deontological ethics (good motives result in good actions), classical liberals highlighted how self-interested behavior (Mandeville's "private vices") may result in positive consequences ("publick benefits"). Classical economists typically favored competition and a capitalist system within representative democracy, but they did not necessarily rule out public regulation or even public provision of services; they were concerned about workers' much lower bargaining power with respect to employers (Adam Smith), and they appreciated the cooperative system (J.S. Mill). During the twentieth century, a much more radical movement emerged, unashamedly pro-market – at times even when there could be no competition – and opposed to any kind of government intervention in the economy. To distinguish their position from classical liberalism, these economists were called "neoliberals," and it is convenient to distinguish at least two main approaches among them (Foucault, 2004).

Neoliberalism, properly called, found its greatest development in the United States, though from there it was exported, for example, to Latin America (Romero Sotelo, 2019). Its ascent was animated by economists of Austrian orientation, above all Hayek and Mises, and it is characterized by the belief that myriad unconnected individual actions produce a spontaneous order through the coordination mechanism of the market. The main political goal of neoliberals is to expand the scope of the market as much as possible and, in parallel, to narrow the reach of the public sector. In economic terms, one can see the ideal of all-pervading markets in the Chicago-style "economic approach" of modeling all human behavior, from the family to organized crime or organ donation, as if it took place in a competitive market. While it has historically been associated with conservatism, this individualist neoliberalism frequently led authors to embrace libertarianism. A relevant example of economic policy supported by this approach is the US Republican Party strategy of "starving the beast:" reducing taxes (especially on the rich) not just in order to enjoy a higher disposable income but also – sometimes primarily – to create public budget deficits that will sooner or later make it necessary to reduce public expenditures, thus attaining the goal of reducing the reach of the government and hopefully creating new private markets in previously publicly dominated sectors.

This approach is different from ordoliberalism, which developed primarily in Germany in the aftermath of World War II, where a national spirit had to be rebuilt and there was international suspicion against a strong German state. The "social market economy" (*soziale Marktwirtschaft*) approach distinguished two modes of public intervention in the economy: in a first stage, the state sets up the social, political, and cultural institutions within which competition can operate and exert its positive effects; in a second stage, the government itself could act as an economic operator, directing the economic processes in one direction or another. According to the ordoliberals, the first kind of intervention is welcome and necessary, but the second is likely to create distortions in the economy and to be counterproductive. The government can thus provide a number of services that create the institutional framework within which the private sector thrives: defense, public order, even health and education. But to do so, it must always try to balance its books: a Keynesian policy of public deficit is likely to overheat the economy and lead to a boom that must ultimately end in a bust. More recent streams of economics in the spirit of ordoliberalism could be the approach of mechanism design and, more in general, the idea that when competition *in* a certain market is impossible – for example, in cases of natural monopoly – the state can usefully intervene to create a competition *for* the market, for example, by giving out monopoly rights in these sectors through public auctions that, if well designed, can provide a second-best alternative in terms of efficiency and public welfare.

These two streams certainly had a hegemonic role in certain periods in some countries. Not by chance, the approach more favorable to public deficits (even if instrumentally and only when they arise from tax cuts) is found in the United States and that praising a balanced budget at any cost is the law in the EU. But neoliberalism and ordoliberalism remain minority orientations, specific subfields so to say, within mainstream economics.

More than wielding substantial power, frequently these schools of thought have been invoked by lobbyists and politicians to justify policies that they wanted to adopt anyway (Fourcade, 2015).

Considered as a whole, mainstream economics is virtually agnostic on policy recommendations: one can find justifications for any economic policy proposal based on mainstream economics. Since the neoclassical synthesis, it has been widely believed that a smart author could push and pull mainstream economics in any direction. Today, as Naidu *et al.* (2019) note, "to produce a consistent model yielding just about any policy recommendation he favored at the start . . . [a] graduate student need not even be that bright!"

Concerning their personal political beliefs, mainstream economists have always had assorted views. Several surveys have found that economists – excluding professors of finance – more frequently self-identify as politically progressive than the average citizen (Cardiff and Klein, 2005). This could reflect the general trend that education is statistically correlated with progressive political views; indeed, faculty members of other disciplines self-identify as progressive more frequently than economics professors. Nonetheless, according to Davis *et al.* (2011), most surveys of US-based economists find that the ratio of Democratic to Republican voters is between 2 and 3 and, in a recent survey of US-based economists, Horowitz and Hughes (2018) find that 58% of respondents agreed that "with laissez-faire policies, economic downturns would be more frequent and more severe," and as many as 70% agreed that "with laissez-faire policies, disparities in wealth would be even greater."

So it is legitimate to ask if Roncaglia (2019) is right in arguing that mainstream economics implies a belief in the invisible hand of the market, at least in principle (even if mainstream economists can always consider "market failures"), or if Hodgson (2019) is right in conversely assuming that heterodox economists share anti-capitalist feelings. In an original survey, De Benedictis and Di Maio (2016) find that indeed there are differences between the two groups, on average. But they rather emphasize the wide variability of opinions. In a survey of Italian economists, they find that an economist's sense of belonging to one or more schools of thought affects her opinions on economic issues in a statistically significant way; however, dichotomous categorizations such as "mainstream vs. heterodox" do not well explain differences of opinion on economic policy proposals.

Rather than emphasizing the average versus the variance of opinions, I think it is important to consider the difference between opinions on economic *issues*, such as the causes of the eurozone crisis, and on policy *proposals*. Concerning the former (and excluding possible exceptions due to axiomatic variation), one of the theoretical cores of mainstream economics is that individuals maximize their goals (utility, profits) by acting in competitive markets. Given their preferences and constraints, if they do not make systematic errors, then the presumption is that the market spontaneously produces an equilibrium in which everybody attains the best result they can – otherwise, they would choose differently in the first place. Mainstream economists who want to say that the market produces inefficient results, then, must either conjure some limitations on the side of the individuals, such as bounded rationality, or they must come up with some "market failures," such as transaction costs or information asymmetry, so that, even if in principle competition would still produce an efficient result, in the specific case under study, it will not.

This way, mainstream economics departs from the premise that the market functions well in its idealized benchmark model. It then splits up into either a "freshwater" front, for example, New Classical macroeconomics, which assumes that the idealized model is more or less applicable to reality, and a "saltwater" front, which considers a collection of instances in which it does not. These two groups diverge so much (both within and between them) on policy prescriptions, that it is hardly surprising that there are no significant differences in the average opinions on policy proposals between them and heterodox economists (who also are very heterogeneous in terms of political ideology). Similarly, in microeconomics, one could think that the ideal perfect competition model roughly represents reality, or one could think that it does not due to the existence of some "market failure." Either way, the burden of proof is on those who wish to carve out a positive role for the public sector against a theoretical benchmark in which government intervention is not needed and produces distortions if applied.

If one starts with the assumption that in principle the market produces efficient outcomes, then policy should primarily aim to remove the barriers to the working of the market in the specific instance, e.g. changing institutions or regulations to bring reality closer to the theoretical model. Only residually, when this is absolutely impossible, should the government be called upon to be directly involved in the economy. As shown in Figure 2.3, mainstream pluralism is wide, but not comprehensive.

## Economics is too hierarchical

Fourcade *et al.* (2015) document that mainstream economists perceive themselves to be at the top of a hierarchy of the social sciences, so they cite political science and sociology papers less often than such disciplines cite economics papers. Most of all, economists created a very steep internal hierarchy, too, as evidenced, for example, by salary inequality among academic economists, the distribution of recognition in their professional associations, and the centralized practice of graduate student placement. For example, let us consider the "pollution theory" of discrimination, which predicts that professions that accrue higher social prestige will not admit women in their ranks, for fear of being downgraded or losing reputation. As Fourcade *et al.* note, in the life sciences and many social sciences, women

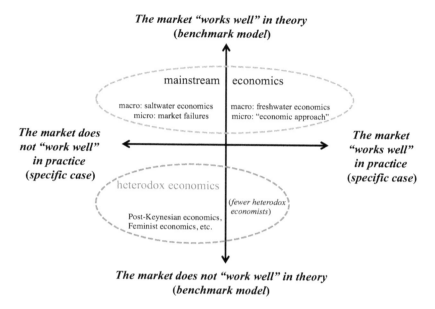

*Figure 2.3* Economics and ideology

have reached or exceeded 50% of doctorates awarded in the United States in the 2000s (60% in sociology and 70% in psychology). In 2010, economics was still hovering around 30%, on a par with the physical sciences. Already Han (2003) had noted that, among all social sciences, there is a correlation between prestige of a department and academic placement of its graduates, but in economics, this correlation is highest.

From a sociological point of view, the difference between economics and other social sciences is that economists more clearly identify with a specific profession, and they more widely share (except the minority of heterodox economists, that is) a scientific paradigm that is assumed to be "true." Fourcade *et al.* (2015) note:[17]

> notwithstanding deep political differences amongst themselves, economists are more likely to think in a strongly integrated and unified framework than other social scientists. For instance, economists agree widely on the core set of principles and tools that structure PhD training. They also rely on textbooks much more than the other social sciences do, including at the graduate level – and graduate textbooks tend to be written by faculty from elite departments.

(p. 96)

These factors facilitate the reproduction of a steep internal hierarchy within the discipline. Such a hierarchy is international: it exhibits the United States at the top, Western countries in descending order, and then emerging and developing countries.

At the top of the pyramid, one channel that shapes this hierarchy is the academic power that accrues to some US economics departments and the top "international" (but actually US-dominated) academic journals. Heckman and Moktan (2018) estimate that, in order to obtain tenure at a top or a middle-ranked US academic institution, only publications in the "top 5" journals count (*The American Economic Review*, *Econometrica*, the *Journal of Political Economy*, the *Quarterly Journal of Economics*, and the *Review of Economic Studies*). The acceptance or rejection of articles by top journals shapes hiring and promotion policies in the lower strata of the pyramid.

This is, again, an international phenomenon. For example, in the Italian case, it was found that publications in lower-ranked journals might damage a candidate more than they help (Corsi *et al.*, 2018), and in a survey on economists in 44 international universities, Powdthavee *et al.* (2017) find that the presence of low-ranking publications in an economist's CV has a damaging effect on her reputation, regardless of her other publications in high-ranking journals.

Around the world, economists tend to think that only what happens at the "top" (however defined) is relevant. This may explain why, in this chapter, I have shown some quantitative trends that differ from what historians of recent economics have claimed (e.g. concerning specialization). Despite their internal differences, economists in the top institutions, who arguably have attracted all the attention, may indeed be more specialized, more frequently leaning to the political center or the right, and possibly more frequently in agreement on policy proposals than the variegated global community of economists that I try to consider here.

There are good reasons for studying what goes on at Chicago or MIT, but not all historiographic and sociological inquiries into contemporary economics should narrowly focus on the top of the profession. First, because academic economics is growing in many countries, thanks to private and public investments in research, and second, because thanks to the increased communication made possible by online tools, previously "hidden" researchers (that is, difficult to reach for Western scholars) have joined the global conversation (dominated by the global North). Accordingly, US-based economists were 56% of the research-active economists (those visible in RePEc) at the beginning of the 1980s, but they accounted for only 26% at the end of the 2010s; in parallel, the proportion of scholars from the EU grew from 23% to 47% in the same period (especially growing in Eastern European countries), and economists from other countries grew from 20% to 26%.

Consequently, we can see a slow trend toward some decentralization of citations in economics. As is well known, typically citations are very unequally distributed, with few papers collecting a very high share of total citations and many papers almost never cited (see next chapter). In economics, too, they are very skewed. But, as shown in Figure 2.4 (panel *a*), the

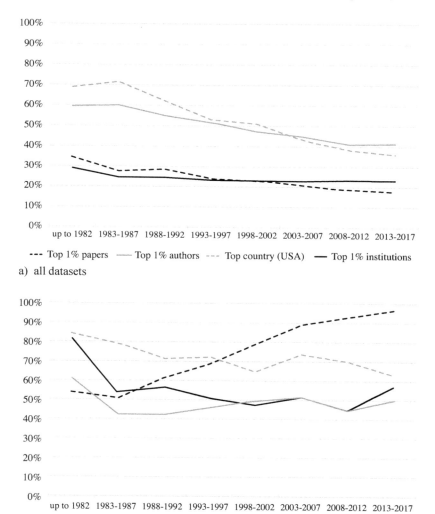

a)  all datasets

b)  from papers published in a top-5 journal

*Figure 2.4* Citations to the top players

share of total citations accruing to the most-cited top 1% of papers, authors, institutions, and countries have all decreased during the period considered. They are still extraordinarily high, but at least the top authors and the top country (the United States) have seen their share of citations almost halved; only the top institutions have better defended their prominent role.

One cannot see this decentralization if focusing on what happens at the top itself. Considering only the citations from papers published in a "top-5" economics journals, the same shares of top papers, authors, institutions, and country are all higher, and they decrease markedly less – some even increase (as shown in panel *b*). Astonishingly, at the end of the 2010s, almost 100% of the works referenced in the top-5 journals are in the top 1% of the most-cited papers.[18] The share of citations from the top-5 journals accruing to US-based economists remains above 60% at the end of the period, and the share of the top-cited authors around 50%. I make no claims here, on the direction of causality in this correlation: papers and authors cited in a top-5 journal become more visible and possibly grow in the rankings. The point is that if one is reading only the top journals, one would get a very narrow idea of the economics literature.

It is an open question to what extent the elite within the profession is self-reproduced by entrenched structures (such as economists' need to economize on their time and selectively choose what to read) or rather by its own behavior, such as "incest" in hiring and promotion (using the term adopted by Heckman and Moktan, 2018). Heckman and Moktan note that in top US departments, there are members of the editorial boards of top-5 journals, who then as faculty members decide on hiring or giving tenure to a young scholar according to her number of publications in a top-5 journal. They can, then, significantly shape personnel selection in their department before a formal procedure even starts. Similarly, Colussi (2018) finds that the institutional dominance of six US departments shapes the selection of journal editors in the top journals; these, once selected, favor authors with whom they have network connections, such as current or former students or faculty colleagues. According to his estimates, in four of the five top journals, roughly half of the articles published have at least an author who has some personal connection with one of the journal editors (e.g. as a colleague, PhD advisor, or coauthor).

These pieces of evidence should not necessarily be interpreted as signs of nepotism; they could represent scientific and cultural cooptation (the problem of low input legitimacy described in the previous chapter). For example, Rodrik (2016, p. 171) recognizes that "because economists go through a similar training and share a common method of analysis, they act very much like a guild." In a comment on his book, Rubinstein (2017, p. 165) replies with a rhetorical question: "why should we expect economists to behave differently than any other group seeking to protect its territory by constructing barriers to entry?"

Rather, as underlined by Heckman and Moktan (2018), the point is that narrowly focusing on the top of the discipline implies a cultural impoverishment due to the small sample size, which makes access to the top prohibitively difficult for scholars not based in the top institutions[19] and due to the narrowness of what is allowed at the top (they report examples of seminal mainstream papers published in lower-ranked journals). We could add that such a focus on the top creates not just a restriction but a bias. The top is not just selective in terms of rigor or quality, but it effectively excludes research from heterodox economists, from those active in smaller research fields or working on "peripheral" economies (who have lower prospects of being cited), and those who choose not to enter or are not allowed into the networks documented by Colussi (2018).

A crucial dimension of the internal hierarchy within economics is that between the higher-ranked, central mainstream and the peripheral, low-ranked heterodox economics. To make an example of this hierarchy, Javdani and Chang (2019) conducted an experiment in 19 countries, polling a large sample of economists on their degree of agreement with a given set of statements about the economy or economic policy. As they randomly misreported the attribution of these statements alternately to notorious mainstream or heterodox economists, they found that the economists interviewed were more often or more strongly in agreement with a statement when it was attributed to a famous mainstream colleague.

It goes without saying that, in the period considered here, there are no heterodox publications in the top journals, but what is more, mainstream journals generally do not cite heterodox ones. Indeed, the mainstream attitude to ignore rather than criticize heterodox contributions is evidenced in the number of citations from mainstream economists to heterodox economists, as a share of the formers' total citations (how many citations the mainstream "imports" from heterodoxy). Conversely, the heterodox economists' engagement with the mainstream can be tracked by the share of citations from heterodox economists to mainstream economists (the mainstream "exports" to heterodoxy). As shown in Figure 2.5, up to the 1980s, heterodox economists captured a not-negligible share of mainstream economists' citations: around 15%, or more than their numbers within the profession. Since then, both the number of heterodox economists and their citations from mainstream colleagues have drastically declined, to below 10%.

In turn, during this period, heterodox economists have focused on entertaining almost unilaterally a debate with the mainstream, quickly reaching a peak of almost 80% of citations from heterodox to mainstream economists; then, in more recent years, they appear to possibly be changing their

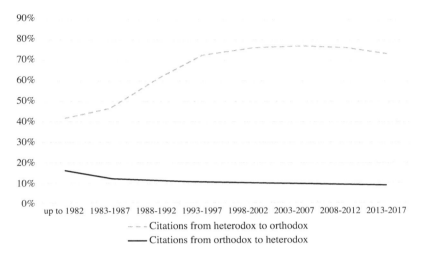

*Figure 2.5* Interchange of citations between mainstream and heterodox economists

approach, slowly starting to cultivate more of an internal conversation (even though mainstream economics still captures the bulk of citations from heterodox scholars). This could reflect the gradual emergence of the process described by Jo *et al.* (2018), of recently increased efforts among heterodox economists to bridge their differences and develop a coherent set of mutually reinforcing research paradigms, instead of focusing on criticizing the dominant approach.

If this trend continues in the future, it will be a positive development. Not because it would contribute to further fragmenting economics but because the obsession with the "top" only impoverishes the potential richness and diversity of economics. New, effective, and low-cost or frequently free tools of disseminating and exchanging economics research, such as RePEc, provide a chance for both mainstream and heterodox economists to enlarge their perspective and become familiar with different methods and viewpoints. This includes a geographical dimension, with the associated chance of "decolonizing" economics.

For example, although as already noted, the share of heterodox economists decreases in virtually all countries, their geographic diffusion becomes more visibly spread out. Over time, heterodox economists have become less heavily concentrated in just a handful of countries, or at least their global visibility has increased in many areas, as shown in Figure 2.6 (comparing two main subperiods in the past half-century). To the extent that an online presence allows for greater opportunities for engagement and debate, we

Share of heterodox economists up to 1997

0.0%    50.0%

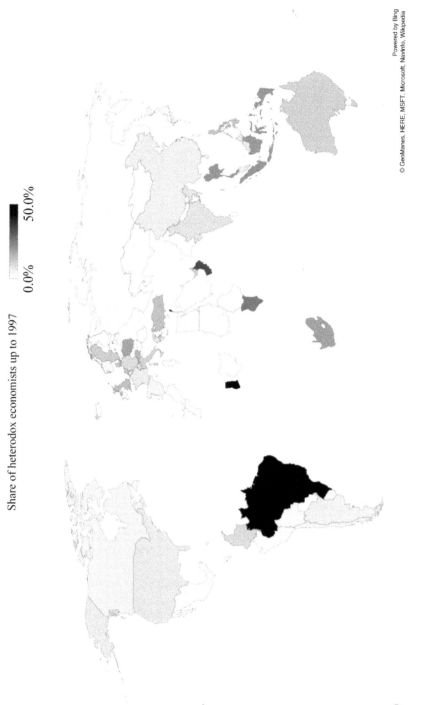

(a)

*Figure 2.6* Geographic diffusion of heterodox economists in two subperiods

Share of heterodox economists since 1998

0.0%    50.0%

(b)

*Figure 2.6* (Continued)

could call this a growth in reach if not in numbers, and a seed for a more pluralist future of economics.

## Notes

1 For details, see Roncaglia (2005).
2 He himself was wary of having an introduction (to be commissioned by the publisher) to the Italian translation of his *General Theory*, writing to Sraffa: "I am not particularly keen on being introduced to the Italian public under the guise of providing a theoretical foundation for all the horrors in the world" (cited in Marcuzzo, 2019).
3 At the time of writing, RePEc contains information on more than 50,000 authors located in more than 100 countries, totaling 2.8 million research works published in 3,200 journals and 5,000 working paper series.
4 Perhaps this is less true the more we look back in the past, but to the extent that today's economists acquire information about scientific publications almost exclusively online, the picture obtained from RePEc will truly represent a "contemporary history" of economics, in Croce's sense.
5 The database contains information on publications from the 1930s onward. Since each working paper series or journal maintainer/publisher provides all the data, which is then handled and organized by a large team of volunteers, I restrict the analysis to the end of 2017 to allow for heterogeneity in the pace of updating the various archives and online material.
6 Steinbaum (2019) responds by noting that economists have always prided themselves on being applied and recurrently of being so for the first time: "in 1964, for example, George Stigler announced that 'the age of quantification is now full upon us,' and called it 'a scientific revolution of the very first magnitude.'"
7 Here, too, we could note that this approach is actually older. Already Wicksteed (1933, p. 3) wrote: "the general principles which regulate our conduct in business are identical with those which regulate our deliberations, our selection between alternatives, and our decisions, in all other branches of life."
8 A bipartition of economics is, of course, a popular interpretation of the economics literature, subscribed to by both many economists and historians of economics (surely by Fine and Milonakis, for example); the originality of Roncaglia's interpretation, besides its comprehensive nature, is the identification of Hayek and Sraffa as the two thought leaders in the respective fields.
9 This partition is increasingly representative: while at the beginning of the 1980s, 75% of publications did not exhibit any JEL code, by the mid-1990s, 80% of publications had at least one, and in the 2010s, more than 99% did. Normally publications have up to three JEL codes, and for simplicity here, I consider up to three codes for each publication.
10 In this work, I always consider five-year periods to allow for delays between writing a paper and having it finally published, as well as delays in economists' reactions to changes in their environment. Because most economists do not publish more than one or two papers per year, considering annual data would amplify very short-term oscillations.
11 For example, an author may specialize in a certain quantitative method only and apply it to a variety of disparate fields. If, then, in the single publication, she uses the JEL codes corresponding to the application only, we would incorrectly infer that she is much less specialized than is really the case.

12 Following the efforts by Fred Lee in the early 2000s, there are now a number of indexes or rankings of heterodox journals; see Corsi *et al.* (2018) for details on the methodology adopted here.

13 "Heterodox economics is a historical science of the social provisioning process . . . The heterodox explanation involves human agency embedded in cultural context and social processes in historical time affecting resources, consumption patterns, production and reproduction, and the meaning (or ideology) of the market, state and non-market/state activities engaged in social provisioning" (*ibid.*, p. 340).

14 A wide range of definitions is collected at www.heterodoxnews.com/hed/

15 "Is our expectation of rain, when we start out for a walk, always more likely than not, or less likely than not, or as likely as not? I am prepared to argue that on some occasions none of these alternatives hold, and that it will be an arbitrary matter to decide for or against the umbrella. If the barometer is high, but the clouds are black, it is not always rational that one should prevail over the other in our minds, or even that we should balance them – though it will be rational to allow caprice to determine us and to waste no time on the debate" (Keynes, 1921, p. 3).

16 This process probably began with the neoclassical synthesis in the Second Postwar period, when economists specialized in what Akerlof (2019) calls "one-deviation-at-a-timism": the production of a vast body of literature based on minor tweaks to a consensus macroeconomic model. Apparently a form of plurality, this approach is actually defined by the strictness with which the rule – just *one* deviation at a time – has been enforced. In the United States, partly in order to expel the old institutionalists from academia, adherence to the horseback macroeconomic model became synonymous with being an economist. Economists who recurrently modified a certain hypothesis had the same benchmark model in mind, as did those who modified a different hypothesis. But with time, this encouraged the creation of separate subfields that, according to some historians of thought, led to specialists in one field becoming unaware of what colleagues were doing in other fields. As I try to show here, it would be more correct to say that economists adapt their founding assumptions and workhorse theories depending on the sub-field in which they are active. Since many authors write in several subfields, this implies that the same author possibly changes her mind even radically, depending on the specific paper she is writing.

17 The remark about the textbook "including at the graduate level" will not be self evident for the economists who are unaware that the typical teaching method of the social sciences is historical and framed in terms of debates between competing views.

18 This does not prove that the top-5 journals exclusively reference the most-cited works, because publications not present in RePEc (notably books) have been excluded from both the numerator and the denominator. However, it is doubtful that articles in the top-5 cite many low cited works that are not indexed in RePEc.

19 Publications in the top-5 journals by authors affiliated with a top US department hover around 50%, with a peak of 74% for the *Quarterly Journal of Economics.*

# 3 What economics could become

The trends in recent economics described in the previous chapter – quantitative explosion but narrowing down in terms of contents, specialization of the publications (if not of the authors), polarization between mainstream and heterodox economics, and invidious hierarchy among and between the two main fronts – could be summarized by saying that economics lacks a wide and fair debate.

There are many reasons for this. Historians of recent economics discussed in the previous chapter have mostly considered reasons internal to the economics debate and to the scientific development of economics: the empirical turn, economics imperialism, and fragmentation.

Another set of reasons for the lack of a fair economics debate has to do with the environment in which economics research is pursued. For example, economists certainly feel (whether they can prove it or not) that social and economic developments are the result of deliberate policies, and these are often implicated by economic theories. Such awareness may have produced a certain drive to conformism, for example, in former Soviet countries. There, many economists and politicians interpreted the fall of the Berlin Wall and the demise of the Eastern bloc as symptoms of the failure of planned economies: several economists saw these developments as a vindication of those approaches to economics that most explicitly advocate for free markets. This has led to academic struggles between younger foreign-educated mainstream economists and the older Marxist powerhouses (for example, in Russia: Zaostrovtsev, 2005). Sometimes, the subsequent failures of deregulation and privatization have been instrumentally used to justify a U-turn toward self-described "heterodox" approaches to economics, which sometimes have little to do with heterodox economics as understood in Western countries and which may be deceptively used to justify unacceptable centralization of economic and political power (Klimina, 2018).

Internationally, professionalization of the discipline has led to a narrowing of its intellectual scope by establishing boundaries with other disciplines and professions. This way, the historical method typical of institutional economics and the German Historical School has slowly developed into economic history, which has then moved closer to history than to economics (until more recently, economic history itself has turned in the direction of mainstream economics, in the guise of "cliometrics": Fine and Milonakis, 2009).

A crucial institutional reason for the narrowing down of the economics debate has to do with the changes in the academic system in general. Its rapid expansion in the second half of the twentieth century has qualitatively changed its nature: from a niche microcosm, almost detached from society and devoted to intellectual debate within a selected elite, academia quickly became an institution of mass education and, in an increasing number of countries, even a commercial enterprise in the market of commoditized higher education. Even where universities remain mostly public or at least not for profit,

> expanded education systems require much more from the public purse, and democratic and other pressures on governments oblige them to account for the expenditures in performance terms. There were demands that universities should serve the needs of the capitalist economy rather than pursue knowledge for its own sake.
>
> (Hodgson, 2011, p. 372)

Hodgson (2011) emphasizes that this change has produced a bias toward specialized teaching aimed at the training of professionals, which in turn has created a new generation of scholars very different from the polymath intellectual of the previous academic age. This may have taken place in the long run, but there is evidence that the sudden enlargement of the university system may have temporarily lowered the barriers to entry for heterodox economists in many countries, including Germany (Heise and Thieme, 2016) and Italy (Pasinetti and Roncaglia, 2006) in the 1960–1970s and Brazil (Fernández and Suprinyak, 2016) in the 1980s–1990s. The temporary reduction in the competitive pressure on the academic job market appears to have led to an increase in diversity among academic economists, which probably benefited in terms of pluralism more than the narrowing of each single scholar's erudition may have hurt it. However, once the enlargement was completed, this dynamic effect (due to the fast-growing demand of professors against a flat supply) has all but disappeared, and the sort of effects considered by Hodgson started to increasingly dominate.

Economics research is not undertaken within academia only (central banks, for example, employ a significant share of economists worldwide), and more in general the funding and organization of research is likely to exert a noticeable impact on the development of economic thought. Funding or lack of it makes the survival of some research centers impossible while allowing for the emergence of new ones; it determines the incentives for research centers to hire and promote certain staff and for institutions and individuals to pursue certain research lines over other ones. The United States has obviously been a main financer of economics research in the second half of the twentieth century, in particular its federal government. There, research funding has been tightly connected to security and military concerns (Mirowski, 2011). In economics, this has led to the accelerated development of operations research (a branch of mathematics devoted to the study of optimal choices or allocations) and the formalization of individual choice models (including in a game-theoretic setting) that in turn have led to the mathematization of the discipline. Within many other countries, the funding of research centers and think tanks has possibly played even a bigger role that I cannot detail here.[1]

These and other impacts have been recognized by historians of economic thought, though their relative relevance is an object of debate. In this chapter, I will focus on a related but separate institutional factor: the introduction of research evaluation schemes. The interest in this specific aspect is that it is a relatively new and understudied international trend and that it is a policy variable increasingly employed around the world and yet whose impact we do not yet fully understand.

Economists are typically interested in regulatory settings and policy levers as useful tools for reaching certain aims, as well as due to the unintended consequences that policies may have. But there is yet scant recognition that, being human beings, economists too, as the idealized economic agents that they study, respond to incentives. When the outcomes of research evaluation are linked to funding decisions or the publicity of competitive rankings, the incentives for scholars and researchers are bound to change. Possibly, with the incentives, this will change the researchers' behavior, too.

Scientists in other disciplines have been more attentive to the issue so far (Rijcke *et al.*, 2016). They have devoted special emphasis to the potential discouragement of radically new path-breaking ideas (Wang *et al.*, 2017), multidisciplinary methods (Rafols *et al.*, 2012; Hicks *et al.*, 2015), and research orientations pursued by a minority of researchers in the respective disciplines (López-Piñeiro and Hicks, 2015).

For example, Hargreaves Heap (2002) finds that the UK system of research evaluation (the Research Assessment Exercise, RAE) has historically incentivized shorter and more applied research projects of an incremental rather than a fundamental kind (that is, refining a research question or looking for new evidence rather than asking a totally new question or questioning some well-established tenet). More in general, the RAE has increased the similarity between the sort of research done in industry and that funded by the public sector. Heap notes that this constitutes a threat for publicly funded research because, if universities do the same work as private companies, then they are possibly no longer entitled to public financing on grounds of their public service.

## A global phenomenon

At one level, there has always been "evaluation" of research in some form. Debating ideas means judging on their relative merits, and for a period, in several languages, "criticizing" was synonymous with investigating. At an even more basic level, intellectuals have always felt the need to discriminate who was worthy of their attention and who wasn't. In most countries, educational institutions must be accredited or anyway allowed to operate by some authority, with the aim of certifying that what is taught and written in these institutions is scientific knowledge and not some form of indoctrination or, worse, fraud. Similarly, individuals may have to certify their credentials in order to access certain science-related professions. And at a deeper level, philosophers have discussed for a few centuries how to demarcate what is "science" and what is not. All these instances do not concern us here, because they either aim at only identifying minimum criteria of demarcation (so one who does not satisfy them is not recognized as a professional economist), or these decisions are based on the idiosyncratic preferences and opinions of the single evaluators.

What is new is the attempt, in the past few decades, to finely categorize each research institution, scholar, scientific journal, or even each publication, establishing its research "quality." Well beyond identifying what is scientific and what not, it is now claimed that we can rank each piece of research in a merit order.

The notion of research "quality" has always been suspect, and with time, the elusive term has increasingly been replaced by the concept of "scientific impact" (which is, however, not usually defined, except by saying that it can be measured by how visible one's research is). Still, quality remains the implicit criterion when the aim is to assess scientific "excellence."

This new fad has at least three defining characteristics: (*i*) it aims at comprehensiveness: in principle, all research could be evaluated, even if in practice one only assesses a sample of research outputs; (*ii*) it aims at fine distinctions of value or worth; and (*iii*) it assumes that research quality (or impact, or excellence) can be measured and compared.

Since schemes of research evaluation are so pervasive, where they are introduced, they exert a systematic impact on all the country's economists (and all scientists in general), and that is why they are so important. The trends mentioned previously (professionalization, expansion of the university system, the demise of the Communist ideology, etc.) likely had heterogeneous impacts across institutions and researchers, whereas formal evaluation schemes that apply uniform rules exert the same sort of impact on everybody who is subject to the scheme in the same way. This is what I mean by saying that they have a *systematic* impact.

To analyze this trend, I collected information on 30 countries in which are based 90.3% of all economists visible on RePEc. As of 2019, 25 of these countries had introduced some form of research evaluation, as shown in Table 3.1, covering 58.4% of all research-active economists. Belgium, Canada, Greece, India,[2] and the United States do not have formal schemes yet, though similar practices are often informally in place. So at least more than half and potentially up to two-thirds of economists are subject to some formal system of research evaluation.[3]

Formal schemes are often in place for the evaluation of research centers or of individuals, for aims of creating rankings (whether complete or singling out "excellence"), hiring or promoting researchers, or allocating funds or defining individuals' pay. The use of systematic research evaluation to reach these goals is less straightforward than it seems.

After being developed on the basis of some indicators, *rankings* take on a life of their own. They end up being considered Swiss army knives that rank the overall "worth" of researchers or universities in general, beyond the purposes for which the ranking was originally developed. Typically, rankings based on the evaluation of the quality of research are often assumed to indicate teaching quality, too. But even more problematic is the logic of ranking individuals or institutions itself. Rankings implicitly assume that research centers are in competition among themselves. They certainly are in some areas for which these rankings are used, for example, in trying to attract new students. But concerning research activities, cooperation is as important as competition, if not more. The relevance of social networks among economists who cooperate with each other despite being based in different institutions has been highlighted for the cases of the United States (Fourcade *et al.*, 2015; Colussi, 2018), Italy (D'Ippoliti, 2018), and other countries. To make an example, the share of articles in RePEc authored by two different economists has increased from 13% at the beginning of the 1980s to 30% at the end of the 2010s and that of articles with three or more authors from 0.6% to more than 10%. Thus, more than 40% of economics articles are now coauthored. It is unclear how these publications can be used to form the ranking of one university (that of one of the authors) in a comparative way relative to all other universities (including those of the coauthors).

The usefulness of research evaluation schemes for *funding* decisions is increasingly criticized, too. Within science policy studies, a near consensus

*Table 3.1* Formalized research evaluation schemes

| | Start year | Object of assessment | Evaluation method in economics | Purpose and uses |
|---|---|---|---|---|
| Turkey | 1981 | Individuals: qualification as ass. or full prof. | Mixed: publications + oral/practical exam | Qualification |
| Mexico | 1984 | Individuals | Bibliometrics + quant. indicators | Rankings, individual remuneration |
| Mexico | 1984 | Universities | Bibliometrics + quant. indicators | Funding, rankings |
| UK | 1986 | Universities: RAE, since 2014: REF | Mixed: informed peer review | Funding, rankings |
| Netherlands | 1987 | Department/schools | Bibliometrics* | Rankings |
| South Africa | 1995 | Universities | Mixed: informed peer review | Funding, rankings |
| Germany | 1998 | Universities (independent NGO) | Mixed: bibliometrics + survey | Rankings (university profiles) |
| Finland | 1998 | Universities (Academy of Finland at irregular intervals) | Mixed: bibliometrics + peer review | Funding, rankings |
| Germany | 2001 | Individuals: qualification as a prof. | Peer review (decentered) | Qualification only |
| China | 2001 | Universities | Bibliometrics | Rankings, individual remuneration |
| Austria | 2002 | Universities | Quantitative indicators (no research outputs) | Funding |
| Austria | 2002 | Individuals: qualification as asst. or ass. prof. | Bibliometrics | Qualification (not mandatory) |
| Switzerland | 2002 | Individuals: qual. as a prof. (German-speaking cantons) | Peer review (decentered) | Qualification only |
| Netherlands | 2003 | Universities | Mixed: bibliometrics + site visit | Rankings |
| Japan | 2003 | Universities | Mixed: complex multi-party system** | Funding, rankings |
| Norway | 2004 | Universities | Bibliometrics | Funding, rankings |
| Germany | 2005 | Universities (government) | Peer review | Funding |
| Italy | 2005 | Universities | Mixed: informed peer review | Funding, rankings |
| Brazil | 2006 | Universities | Mixed: informed peer review | Rankings |
| France | 2007 | Individuals: qualification as asst. or full prof. | Peer review: CV + interview | Hiring, promotion |
| France | 2007 | Universities; since 2014: HCERES | Mixed: bibliometrics + site visit | Funding, rankings |

(*Continued*)

*Table 3.1* (Continued)

| | Start year | Object of assessment | Evaluation method in economics | Purpose and uses |
|---|---|---|---|---|
| Spain | 2007 | Individuals: qualification as asst., ass., or full prof. | Mixed: publications + interview | Qualification only*** |
| Sweden | 2009 | Universities | Bibliometrics | Funding |
| Denmark | 2009 | Universities | Bibliometrics | Funding |
| Australia | 2010 | Universities | Mixed: informed peer review | Funding |
| Italy | 2012 | Individuals: qualification as asst., ass., or full prof. | Mixed: informed peer review | Qualification only |
| Slovakia | 2013 | Universities | Mixed: informed peer review | Funding |
| Poland | 2013 | Universities | Bibliometrics | Funding |
| Croatia | 2013 | Universities | Bibliometrics | Funding |
| Korea | 2014 | Universities | Mixed, but no eval. of research outputs | Funding, rankings |
| Portugal | 2015 | Universities | Peer review | Funding |
| Sweden | 2016 | Universities | Peer review | Funding |
| Turkey | 2016 | Universities | Peer review | Rankings |

*Notes*: countries are sorted by their first introduction of a formal evaluation scheme (excluding accreditation systems).

* In 2015, in the Netherlands, the criterion of publication volume was abolished.

** In Japan, university assessment makes use of performance metrics and qualitative evaluation.

*** In Spain, the number of qualifications (habilitación) awarded has been limited so far, so that practically, being qualified is equivalent to being promoted.

has emerged in recent years that concentrating funding of research on excellence (however defined) is not a sensible idea. Beside the sheer riskiness of truly innovative research, there are several reasons for caution. According, for example, to Fortin and Currie (2013), in many disciplines, there are decreasing returns to scale, so that each additional dollar spent on a same project yields lower benefits than the previous one. Gross and Bergstrom (2019) highlight that the activity of picking the winners is costly: both directly for the evaluation agency and indirectly for the system as a whole (researchers must spend time writing proposals instead of doing science, and referees or panel members must devote time to evaluating, etc.) and therefore any potential benefit over random or uniform funding must be assessed against these costs. In practice, "picking winners" is not easy, either: its effectiveness could vary by country (Sandström and Van den Besselaar, 2018) and small networks of elite players could capture the funding system (Ma *et al.*, 2015).

And yet picking a few excellence centers is less difficult than attempting to fine-tune funding to the detailed results of a comprehensive research assessment scheme. If one has to develop a whole ranking, the risks of errors cumulate and small changes in the ranking methodology can produce widely different results (see e.g. Corsi *et al.*, 2011).[4] Nonetheless, as shown in Table 3.1, funding is the most common aim of formal research evaluation schemes.

Scholars have criticized the link of research evaluation with funding decisions. Using the example of research in cervical cancer, Gillies (2014) shows that traditional methods of research evaluation for funding decision purposes favor mainstream research programs against minority research programs, which leads to the stifling of new ideas and of innovation. For these reasons and some more, such as fostering pluralism and seeking a diversification of the grant portfolio, an increasing number of science funders have started experimenting with the introduction of random elements in their grant selection procedures. Supporters of this option have it that elements of randomness reduce the bias that plagues grant-giving when it is associated with research evaluation (see next section) and that they improve diversity among grantees, foster a humbler approach among scientists, and reduce the costs of grant application and evaluation (Adam, 2019).

These examples aim at showing that systematic and comprehensive research assessment schemes are not necessarily as useful as they may appear (unless, that is, their explicit aim is to control and shape research activities in a country).

This is not to say that researchers should be unaccountable. In many countries, they are civil servants and thus, as Hodgson (2011) notices, they must justify their claim on the public purse. For example, Marcuzzo and

Zacchia (2010) highlight that still in the 1990s and early 2000s in Italy, there were several academic economists with apparently no publications for several consecutive years. One could discuss what a meaningful minimum academic productivity that can be expected from public employees is, but it is likely to be greater than zero. However, to identify the neglectful "free-riders," we don't need overly complex algorithms of pervasive research evaluation: zero will be zero by the most basic metrics, and there is no need to assign precise values to all other researchers (or even to talk about the quality of their work) to distinguish their efforts from zero. It is one thing to try to identify inactive researchers; it is another thing to try to finely measure such an elusive concept as the quality of research.

When an explicit aim of science and research policy is to foster pluralism, the risk of formal and centralized research evaluation schemes is to speed up the process of homologation within each discipline. By contrast, decentered and informal systems in principle allow for more variety across research institutions, to experiment with local approaches to how to evaluate the candidates to hire or promote, and how to define the sort of research outputs the production of which each institution wishes to encourage. It is necessary to specify that they allow for more variety "in principle" only because, as Heckman and Moktan (2018) show for the case of the United States, informal rules can be as binding as formal ones when they are consistently adhered to by a whole community.[5] It is therefore an empirical matter, of which we will only have evidence in the long run, which sort of system more strictly enforces uniformity and which instead allows for more pluralism between the formal and the informal ones. There is, however, little doubt that formal systems have a high potential for systematically shaping research due to the uniform pressure they exert, which leaves no room for heterogeneity even in principle.

A large stream of literature on the science of science has investigated the unintended consequences of research evaluation in terms of inducing scientific malpractice and professional fraud (for the case of economics, see Necker, 2014). However, in keeping with the approach taken in the first chapter, I will not focus on this aspect: bad faith among the economists is not a necessary assumption to show that research evaluation can have negative impacts on the economics debate.[6] Instead, I will focus on the bias implicit in these systems: introduced by law or in the way these systems are implemented in practice.

## Bias and discrimination in research evaluation

Scientists and policymakers discuss many aspects of if and how to evaluate research. A relevant topic is, for example, what to evaluate: while the evaluation of individuals or research centers is widespread (see Table 3.1), some countries, such as the Netherlands, have a tradition of evaluating research projects, as have many science funders. In the latter cases, evaluation is typically ex ante, although ex post reports and audits are not rare. In the context of ex ante evaluation for funding decisions, a well-known problem is that if the evaluation of an investigator's previous research enters the decision on new funding lines, then cumulative divergence between "superstar" researchers and all others quickly accumulates (Bol *et al.*, 2018). Beside removing all pretense of a level playing field in the scientific discussion, the problem of this practice is that it creates a lock-in of scientific research programs that may stifle innovation. This is all the more relevant in light of the intrinsic uncertainty of research, which implies that the best ideas ex ante, not always ex post translate into the best research findings and therefore prestigious publications. It is thus unfair to penalize researchers for their past lost bets.

Concerning how research evaluation may impact the contents and development of science, with which we are concerned here, the most debated issue in the literature is not what to evaluate, but how. A wide debate focuses on the respective advantages of bibliometric methods and peer review.[7]

Focusing on economics, Corsi *et al.* (2019) distinguish two dimensions of bias of these methods: on diversity of backgrounds, and on diversity of ideas.

Especially in the most recent years, the impact of research evaluation on diversity of backgrounds has mostly been studied with reference to gender equality. It is a relevant case per se, as well as because several findings in terms of gender-based discrimination highlight potential risks of discrimination for other minorities or researchers in precarious positions too, such as younger untenured academics, those belonging to racial or ethnic minorities, and so on. The point is especially topical in economics, for in most countries, economics exhibits the highest gender gaps in academic tenure and promotion rates, as well as in average salaries and job satisfaction, with respect to both the social sciences and several math-intensive fields (Bayer and Rouse, 2016).[8]

The two debates, that on diversity of backgrounds and that on pluralism of scientific paradigms, are not disconnected. First, because discrimination against minority backgrounds shows that current methods of research evaluation are not as objective as claimed by evaluation agencies (unless one is ready to claim, in the face of their systematically lower ratings, that women and minorities are worse researchers). And second, because there is empirical evidence that women and other minorities hold specific views. In the case of economics, surveys have found systematic differences between men's and women's research interests and economic policy preferences (e.g. May *et al.*, 2018). It could thus be the case that increasing diversity of backgrounds could bring about higher diversity of scientific perspectives, too (e.g. Forget, 1995). However, some authors consider this second point an essentialist argument, if taken to imply a causal relation whereby more women in academia would automatically translate into greater diversity of views. For example, Zacchia (2017) finds that a progressively more competitive environment in the last few decades induced women economists to adopt a strategy of homologation toward the same research interests of their male colleagues in order to increase their chances to achieve a tenured academic position. Therefore, it is important to consider not simply the share of women (or other minorities) that positively qualify within a certain research assessment system but also to look at the profile of these successful women.

In any case, it is convenient to distinguish the two debates, because discrimination against minority backgrounds is a problem common to all disciplines (though possibly to different degrees), whereas discrimination against minority viewpoints and approaches depends on the intellectual landscape of each discipline (even if it can appear, in different guises, in all disciplines).

Concerning diversity of backgrounds, fairness in terms of gender equality has increasingly been investigated within the literature on the bias of peer review (Marsh *et al.*, 2009, 2011). In most cases, empirical evidence is sought in contexts of grant applications and/or journal article submissions, because information on the outcomes of nationwide research evaluation schemes is generally unavailable. The assumption is usually that any bias found (or not) in the peer review process in one context may be present in other contexts, too.

One problem with studying peer review is that it is often anonymous, making it impossible for researchers to consult public datasets on referees' and applicants' sex and other background characteristics. Perhaps as a consequence, results have been mixed and often country specific or discipline specific (Tamblyn *et al.*, 2018). A meta-analysis of 21 studies on peer review within funding grant applications found that men have greater odds of receiving grants than women, by about 7% (Bornmann *et al.*, 2008). But Marsh *et al.* (2009) used a more sophisticated statistical method on the same data, finding no significant gender effect. In the case of journal article submissions, a common finding is that editors select more male reviewers, and this pattern is more pronounced for male editors (Primack *et al.*, 2017). This seems to be due to a predominance of male senior active researchers, combined with more invitations going to senior researchers. However, women also show a slightly higher propensity to decline invitations to review.

In many instances, the apparent predominance of male reviewers of journal article submissions does not seem to lead to higher rejection rates for female authors (Lerback and Hanson, 2017). In contrast, Murray *et al.* (2018) find a small but statistically significant advantage for men authors within the peer review of 7,192 submissions to the biosciences journal *eLife*. They find that such gender inequity was greatest when the team of reviewers was all male, while mixed-gender teams lead to more equitable peer review outcomes.[9]

Bagues *et al.* (2017) follow this line of research in one of the few studies on the outcomes of nationwide evaluation schemes of individual researchers. They consider the procedures to obtain a qualification as associate or full professor in Spain and in Italy: these qualifications are necessary requirements to find employment in academia in the two countries. Bagues *et al.* find that female evaluators are not significantly more favorable toward female candidates, and actually male evaluators become less favorable toward female candidates when they are part of mixed-gender committees. More women evaluators could thus turn out to even damage women's chances as candidates.

One of the elements considered by Bagues *et al.* is the existence of personal or professional links between the candidates and the commissioners; they find that these network connections matter for obtaining a qualification. This could be one of the causes of women's worse professional outcomes, since there is evidence that they are less fully integrated into professional networks than their male colleagues. However, Corsi *et al.* (2019) have run the same analysis for the case of economics in Italy, finding that once controlling for the topics and methods of research (diversity of ideas), the impact of network connections is no longer statistically significant. Again, it seems conformism is empirically a bigger threat for academia than corruption.

Finally, experimental evidence has resulted in equally mixed results so far. Knobloch-Westerwick *et al.* (2013) report that publications ostensibly authored by male authors were associated with greater perceived quality within a large sample of communication scholars, in particular if the topic was considered typically "masculine." In contrast, Williams and Ceci (2015) find that in the STEM (science, technology, engineering, and mathematics) fields, faculty members even appear to positively discriminate in women's favor, though interestingly not in the case of economics.

In conclusion, it is fair to say that there are strong clues of possible discrimination against women and other minorities within peer review processes but no conclusive evidence yet.

In the face of these clues, and in order to reduce the cost of research evaluation, an increasing number of countries decided to turn to bibliometric indicators (compare Table 3.1), that is, quantitative measures of research outputs. These are typically indexes based on the quantity and kind of publications, interpreted as measures of productivity, or based on citation counts, interpreted as measures of visibility within the scientific community.

It is frequently held that by being defined ex ante and independently of the specific person (or publication) under evaluation, by design, bibliometric indicators remove *direct discrimination*, that is, the unfair application of different standards to similar cases. For example, taking advantage of their role as commission members, Jappelli *et al.* (2017) analyzed a nondisclosed sample of publications evaluated with both bibliometric methods and peer review within a recent research quality evaluation exercise in Italy. They find that bibliometric evaluation does not penalize women with respect to men, while peer review might, and that in general, bibliometric evaluation proves to be more favorable to women than peer review, independently of the reviewers' sex.

However, it is often found that bibliometric methods bring about issues of *indirect discrimination*, that is, the unfair application of uniform rules to different cases. From a gender perspective, a crucial issue is that women publish fewer articles on average, partly because of heavier teaching and administrative burdens (documented e.g. by Baccini *et al.*, 2014). There is also evidence that men engage more in self-citing (for the case of economics: Ferber and Brün, 2011) and that, more in general, publications with female authors receive fewer citations on average, even after controlling for author and publication characteristics (Abramo *et al.*, 2015).

A specific problem in applying bibliometric indicators is that, in practice, journal-level indexes rather than publication-level metrics are used. For some reason, this is especially frequent in economics. Studies have demonstrated that journal ratings are the strongest predictor of the results obtained in the United Kingdom's 2008 Research Assessment Exercise (Brooks *et al.*, 2014), as well as in the subsequent Research Excellence Framework (REF; Stockhammer *et al.*, 2017). Similarly, Corsi *et al.* (2018) find that a government-determined list of "A-ranked" journals crucially shaped the results of the national qualification system (the ASN, from the Italian acronym), even though the number of articles published in journals ranked in this list was only one among several mandated criteria. The UK and Italian cases are especially interesting because in the REF and ASN, bibliometric indicators were not in principle the main method of evaluation. These schemes were rather based on "informed peer review," that is, a peer review process in which reviewers are provided with quantitative data (for example, on Journal Impact Factors or candidates' citation counts) ostensibly only to help in their decision. At least in the case of economics, the UK and Italian experiences show that with this method, bibliometric data tend to take on decisive weight over all other criteria and considerations: in economics, informed peer review is de facto bibliometrics.

Crucially, this happens whenever the objects of evaluation are published pieces of research, even if quantitative data are not explicitly provided to the referees. The journal name suffices in these cases – especially in economics, where top journals carry the prestige and reputation of top US departments, as noted in the previous chapter. The use of journal rankings has been criticized, for example, because the distribution of citations is highly skewed, making journal-level averages no indication of the visibility (let alone quality) of the single papers published in the journal (Moed, 2005). This issue, too, is relevant from the point of view of diversity of backgrounds, because for some reason, there are systematic differences in the average ranking of journals in which men and women predominantly publish (e.g. for the UK case: Brooks *et al.*, 2014).

Overall, the evidence of biases in bibliometric indexes appears to be more clear cut than that on peer review. In part as a response to these pitfalls, as mentioned, the United Kingdom introduced a system based on informed peer review. In the Dutch scheme, the set of indicators was modified in 2015, excluding the sheer volume of publications (which further provides toxic incentives, as discussed subsequently). In Italy, regulation considers bibliometric indexes appropriate for certain disciplines (mostly the natural and life sciences) and reserves peer review for other disciplines (the humanities and social sciences).

However, economists globally continue to make significant use of bibliometric indicators when acting as reviewers of funding bodies or within research evaluation schemes, and there still seems to be widespread belief in the profession that citation metrics can and should be used to measure researchers' value (Hamermesh, 2018). It is thus worth investigating the role of these metrics in greater detail, before discussing the impact of research evaluation schemes on the diversity of viewpoints.

## The trouble with citation metrics

Bibliometric indexes based on various ways of counting and aggregating citations are increasingly applied to the evaluation of individuals, journals, departments, universities, and even whole countries. There is a general consensus that these indexes are better suited to measure visibility within a certain field in the natural sciences than in the social sciences and humanities, but economics has always aspired to be considered akin to the natural sciences (Mirowski, 1992) and does not seem to miss the chance in this case, too. As shown in Table 3.1, in the majority of countries where formal evaluation systems exist, bibliometrics is the only or a main evaluation method in economics. Where evaluation is not centralized and formal, such as in the United States and Canada, informal journal rankings are widely used.

Even in the natural sciences, the use of these metrics is not noncontentious. A growing number of researchers, journals, associations, and scientific societies distance themselves from these practices (e.g. the International Mathematical Union, the International Council of Industrial and Applied Mathematics, and the Institute of Mathematical Statistics: Adler *et al.*, 2008) or at least voice the need for better, unbiased metrics and a more balanced, prudent, and self-aware use of them (see e.g. the San Francisco Declaration on Research Assessment, DORA; the Leiden Manifesto for research metrics: Hicks *et al.*, 2015; or the joint declaration by the Académie des Sciences, Leopoldina and Royal Society, 2018).

Citation metrics raise two sorts of debates in the literature: one empirical, regarding their technical use, and one theoretical, regarding their meaning and, more generally, the meaning of scientific "quality," visibility, or impact.

From an empirical standpoint, the first challenge is that citation counts are easily found to be skewed and biased, in the sense that they correlate with many things besides quality (for a review, see D'Ippoliti, 2018). To mention just some known problems, citations are found to correlate with the language and kind of publication, the reputation of the journal or outlet, and even with title length or the fact that the title contains a hyphen; citations further depend on the authors' seniority, their field and degree of specialization, and gender, and systematic differences are found in the average citations of different disciplines or even between subfields of a discipline.

For example, in economics, citations are systematically higher in econometrics and lower in the history of economic thought, mostly as a consequence of the relative size of the two communities of scholars but also due to different citation habits. As a consequence, the use of citation metrics in which citation counts are not normalized implies strong value judgments on the relative worth of disparate methods and fields of research. That is why some authors (e.g. in economics Corsi *et al.*, 2010, 2011) propose the standardization of indexes by subfield and/or other author or publication characteristics.

The typical distribution of citations is problematic as well: not only is it highly asymmetric, making average values virtually meaningless, but it also exhibits fat tails, implying, for example, that within the same journal, it is not strange to find both an extraordinary number of papers that are never cited and a considerable number of works that are cited many times more than what many believe would be explained by their intrinsic quality. These findings are typically associated with the "Matthew effect," that is, the growing polarization whereby works that are highly cited are more likely to be further cited.

The second debate, as mentioned, concerns the theoretical and conceptual problem of understanding what citations really measure. Jeroen Bosman

$(2007)^{10}$ has proposed a scheme of interpretation that recognizes that citations depend on several crucial characteristics of a work. Freely regrouping and modifying some, we may distinguish at least three classes of factors:

- *availability* of a work: this will depend on ease of access (e.g. online presence, paywalled or open access publication, etc.), libraries and other players' actions (ranking and indexing services, databases, etc.), and the authors' promotion of their publication;
- *attractiveness* of the publication: depending at least on the language, quality of the metadata (clarity of the abstract, catchiness of the title, salience of the keywords, etc.), writing style, alerting and marketing services of the publication outlet, and prestige of the authors and outlet;
- *citability*: depending at least on the topic; the fact that the work contains a review of the literature or original research; that the author belongs to certain networks; that the findings of the work support or contradict the citers' own findings; and finally, among other elements, the quality of the work.

Quality is just one among several determinants of citations, and these determinants may change over time. For example, with reference to one of the elements listed in the third group, whether the findings of a cited work support or contradict the citing author's own findings, Seabrooke *et al.* (2015) have carried out an interesting study on how this impacts citation behavior in economics. They analyzed the citation network of the debate about fiscal policy on the *American Economic Review*, finding a high share of negative citations (sign that a real discussion was ongoing) as well as many neutral, so-to-say descriptive citations, in the period 1969–1974. By contrast, in the more recent 2009–2014 period, citations have become overwhelmingly positive. Seabrooke *et al.* comment: "positive affirmation of existing economic thinking is much more apparent. This may be a consequence of the increased production of economic knowledge, but nevertheless points to a change in what can be contested within the economics profession" (p. 13).

Many scholars have investigated whether there is a growing importance of strategic considerations in authors' citing behavior, for example, in terms of trying to please colleagues who are likely to act as a journal's referees. Empirical investigations of individual citers' motives usually reflect ambivalence in citations. Studies find that both intellectual and "ceremonial" motivations drive citation behavior. For example, White and Wang (1997) have surveyed two samples of 25 and 15 agricultural economists; they quote researchers reporting about citations in their published works: "we didn't want to be told we had neglected to cite certain people. So there are people in here, for example, X is one of these people we anticipated being a referee" (p. 145); or

> [i]n economics there are all different kinds of levels of journals, and the theoretical level that we were aiming at is most closely matched by the *Journal of Economic Theory*, *Review of Economic Studies*, and *Econometrica*. The paper that we actually wrote was ultimately submitted to *Econometrica*. So, when we picked out references, we tried to stay in that group. It is a little bit of gamesmanship in a way, to be citing the right people.
>
> (p. 136)

In the case of Italy-based economists, D'Ippoliti (2018) shows that social network dynamics, such as being coauthors, working in the same institutions, or publishing in the same journals, significantly affect the probability that two economists cite each other, as does their sharing a similar political ideology. Moreover, these social connections do not cancel out in the aggregate, and an author's total number of accumulated citations depends on her position in terms of network centrality. For example, for younger economists, it is better to start their careers in a large department, in order to have many colleagues who in the next few years are more likely to cite one's works. For women, in particular, it appears to be profitable, with the aim of accumulating citations, to stand in a bridging role (having high betweenness centrality) in the network of political-ideological orientations. For everybody, a safe bet is to work on topics that are not too distant from what the bulk of the profession specializes in.

These social determinants of citations do not worry authors who claim that citations are good measures of scientific quality. For example, without denying the social component of citation behavior, Moed (2005) argues that citations reflect both intellectual and social prestige at the same time:

> In any field there are leading groups active at the forefront of scientific development. Their leading position is both cognitively and socially anchored. Cognitively, their important contributions tend to be highlighted in a state-of-the-art of a field. But *to the extent that the science system functions well* in stimulating and warranting scientific quality, leading groups, and particularly their senior researchers, tend at the same time to acquire powerful social positions.
>
> (p. 219, italics added)

In his view, thanks to the efficiency of science, there is an indirect channel whereby even perfunctory citations ultimately reflect the scientific achievement of the cited person. Reliance on this indirect channel, though, rests on the assumption that science is in fact organized in a way that rewards scientific achievement by conferring prominent social positions to the individuals who contribute most to the scientific development of their field, and to them only. Ultimately, the opinion on what citations measure depends on one's views on the working of the science industry. That is why it is crucial to recall that science is a human endeavor affected by external social dynamics, as discussed in Chapter 1, and that the economics debate is far from resembling an efficient "marketplace of ideas" where schools and scholars compete on a level playing field.

## Consequences of research evaluation in economics

The same biases of research evaluation found in terms of diversity of backgrounds have been found when considering diversity of viewpoints and methods, too. It has been noted for all disciplines that national research assessments tend to reward the approaches that are more visible and popular within the discipline, reinforcing the pre-existing journal rankings and more in general the discipline's hierarchy. In economics, there is evidence that evaluation systems are purposely employed to that end.

It has been documented that an active majority of economists make use of biased methods of research evaluation in order to police the field and establish the absolute dominance of their preferred scientific paradigm, the mainstream, to the detriment of heterodox economics. Studies have focused on Anglo-Saxon countries (e.g. on the United Kingdom: Harley and Lee, 1997; Lee, 2006; Lee *et al.*, 2013; on the United States, which, however, has an informal system: Fourcade *et al.*, 2015; and on Australia: Bloch, 2010), German-speaking countries (Grimm *et al.*, 2018), France (Chavance and Labrousse, 2018), and Italy (Corsi *et al.*, 2010, 2011, 2018).

In several countries, this discussion intersects that on the use of journal rankings, because these lists tend to be extremely biased towards the mainstream (Lee *et al.*, 2013; Corsi *et al.*, 2018). However, both bibliometrics and peer review–based systems seem to produce similarly negative impacts in terms of pluralism and diversity of viewpoints. The issue here seems to be that mainstream economists are a majority of the discipline and therefore have both higher citation indexes and a greater probability to be called to act as referees. This would not be a problem, per se, were it not that, lacking explicit rules that protect minority approaches, in many countries, the presumption seems to have prevailed that in economics, "different" really means "inferior."

For example, at the end of his mandate as commissioner within the first Italian evaluation scheme, Luigi Pasinetti reported on his experience trying to reach a consensus with his mainstream colleagues:

> Cases like the following was the first cause of my denying consensus (without any effect, being always in a minority). Quality of the product:

"This paper is published in a top field journal, the IF of the journal is high, hence the paper is excellent" or conversely (always on quality of the paper) "this paper is published in my opinion in a non serious journal [in the specific case of this quotation it was the *Journal of Post Keynesian Economics*], hence the quality is limited." Notice that the evaluation I am referring to is on quality, not on internationalization of the product!

(Pasinetti, 2006, p. 5)

However, diversity of viewpoints is not limited to the mainstream-heterodox divide. Corsi *et al.* (2018) highlight the negative effects of research evaluation practices on economists' engagement in the history of economic thought, possibly due to the fact that this subfield is not based on mathematical models and relies on multidisciplinary approaches. More in general, the various subfields of economics have different preferred dissemination outputs (i.e. more books and book chapters in the history of economic thought and nearly exclusive reliance on journal articles in econometrics); researchers active in the different fields of economics have different research interests and preferences for interdisciplinary approaches; and the various fields are made up of scientific communities of various sizes.

As a consequence, it is not only the heterodox who think that economics lacks a fair and wide debate. A recent survey by the American Economic Association (AEA) among its members has found that as many as 21% of respondents feel their "ideas and opinions are often ignored within the field of economics" (Allgood *et al.*, 2019), and 16% have felt discriminated against or treated unfairly at least once based on their research topics. This is the highest value after discrimination based on sex (17%), and, actually, discrimination based on research is the second most frequent ground of complaint among women economists (23%), being even more diffused among them than feelings of discrimination based on marital status. Similarly, among non-whites, it is the second most frequent ground of discrimination (20%) after race, even before sex. Among males, it is the most frequent form of discrimination (13%), on a par with place of employment.

In turn, discrimination based on place of employment could highlight the steep internal hierarchy among economists underlined by Fourcade *et al.* (2015), who stress the overlapping of place-based and ideological hierarchy within the discipline. Significantly, Allgood *et al.* (2019) report that, even though the survey was aimed at collecting evidence on diversity of backgrounds, many interviewed economists decided to complete a final open question in order to raise the issue of pluralism:

There was . . . a set of comments (about 110) opining that economics is not open to heterodox approaches or views, or that in general there is a small set of fields within economics that matter. If you are not in one of these fields, or do not use the prescribed research methods, you are not taken seriously. The impact can stifle the profession. . . .

This last comment ties into what was likely the second largest theme in the written responses (about 250 comments). There was a frequent reference to the elitism within the field. There is a strong sense that the AEA, the NBER, and the top journals – and de facto the profession – are controlled by economists from the top institutions.

(p. 29)

In this context, what centralized research evaluation schemes apparently did in many countries is to provide a State-sanctioned tool to reinforce the discipline's internal hierarchy.

In looking for common international trends, we can compare a country's average performance on RePEc before and after the introduction of a formal system of research evaluation. At this stage, it is unnecessary to distinguish between bibliometrics-based and peer review–based systems: based on the existing evidence, both seem to negatively impact the diversity of viewpoints.[11]

To capture the specificity of countries that introduced these systems, it is appropriate to normalize all data by the world average in order to control for the general time trends described in the previous chapter (for example, the phenomenon of "citation inflation"). Figure 3.1 reports the dynamics of average productivity, measured by the number of unique works per author; the average visibility, measured by the citations received, standardized by year of publication (because more recent papers have had less time to be cited); and the share of heterodox economists in the country. All series are considered before and after the introduction of formal evaluation schemes and are expressed as ratios of the respective world averages in each period. Since in many populous countries, these schemes were introduced during the 2000s, it seems appropriate to consider variations before and after ten years from the introduction of the formal scheme: a wider time window would sensibly reduce sample size.

It emerges that countries that introduced formal systems usually started from relatively low levels of productivity and visibility, with levels between 65% and 85% of the world average 10 years before introducing the research evaluation scheme. They then experienced a significant growth until overcoming the world average in terms of productivity, by around 5%, and narrowing the gap in terms of citations, reaching 85% of the world average. In addition to the risk of falling into a "post hoc, ergo propter hoc" fallacy, these results should be interpreted with caution because change obviously takes time. To start with, the world average itself moves, as countries that do not adopt formal evaluation schemes have also typically accepted the competitive

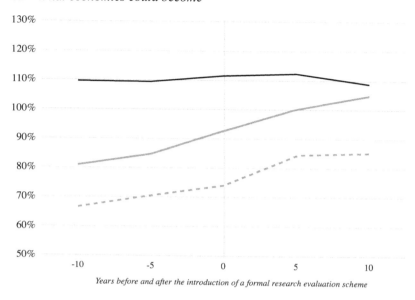

130% ·······································
120% ·······································
110% ·······································
100% ·······································
90% ·······································
80% ·······································
70% ·······································
60% ·······································
50% ·······································
        -10        -5         0         5         10

*Years before and after the introduction of a formal research evaluation scheme*

‒ ‒ Relative citations per author    —— Relative works per author    ▬ Relative share of heterodox economists

*Figure 3.1* Average visibility, productivity, and share of heterodox economists:
countries that introduced a formal research evaluation scheme relative to
the world average

logic of boosting scientific productivity and visibility. For the countries that
adopt formal schemes, improvement over a moving target is more difficult.

More in general, the trends in productivity and visibility shown in Figure 3.1 are gradual: there is a catching up of the countries that introduced a
formal research evaluation scheme, but it begins before the start of formalized evaluation. This anticipated effect could be due to the fact that such
schemes are not the key to raising productivity and visibility; that in most
countries they have been amply announced in advance and only slowly
implemented (and researchers adapted already after the announcement);
or, finally, that the setup of such schemes could signal a more general process of restructuring of the research sector in a certain country, which could
have started before the introduction of formal research evaluation.

Considering the impact on the share of heterodox economists, it emerges
that the countries that introduced formal schemes tend to exhibit higher-
than-average shares of heterodox economists, by around 10 percentage
points of the world average, both before and after the scheme is introduced.
This share remains roughly stable over the period, with a reduction of
around 4 percentage points of the world average between five and ten years

after the introduction of a formal scheme. Indeed, a smaller and delayed impact in this case is to be expected, because these schemes typically affect hiring and promotion procedures and do not typically imply that currently employed economists are expelled from the profession. Moreover, although this reduction is – for the moment – very small, it should be recalled that the share of heterodox economists worldwide has also been falling in the past few decades: the reduction has just been quicker where research evaluation has been institutionalized.

More sophisticated analyses would require a larger sample of observations: still relatively few economists have been subject to a formal evaluation scheme for more than 10 years. However, let us accept for the sake of the argument that by expelling "low-performing" economists from the profession, the countries that introduced formal schemes were increasingly able to catch up and actually improve their productivity and visibility metrics with respect to the world average. Even such an argument would have to consider that mainstream economists "perform better" than heterodox economists only in a very nuanced sense.

As shown in Figure 3.2, until the beginning of the 1990s, heterodox economists exhibited comparable levels of citations per capita (panel *a*), though with a considerably greater variability among them. Then, both mainstream and heterodox economists partook in the process of citation inflation, but the mainstream benefited slightly more from it (while the variance among heterodox economists collapsed). At the end of the 2010s, the difference in average citations accruing to the two groups is statistically significant but very small. It alone cannot justify the increase by 30 percentage points of the world average (almost a 40% relative increase) in the citations received by the economists in countries that introduced formalized research evaluation.

In terms of productivity, the opposite takes place: heterodox economists were as productive as their mainstream colleagues until the end of the 1990s, and then, while both groups started publishing more, heterodox economists actually become more productive than mainstream economists. This finding could be evidence of a defense strategy among the heterodox, who may have tried to compensate for the lower quality of their output as perceived by their mainstream colleagues with a greater number of outputs.

In conclusion, preliminary evidence suggests that some of the worrying phenomena that plague current economics, namely the shrinking share of heterodox economists and the single-minded focus on increasing citations and publications, developed even faster in the countries that introduced some form of formalized research evaluation system than in those that rely on informal systems.

Overall, that formalized evaluation schemes may induce an increase in citations is not necessarily a matter of concern, except that this will further

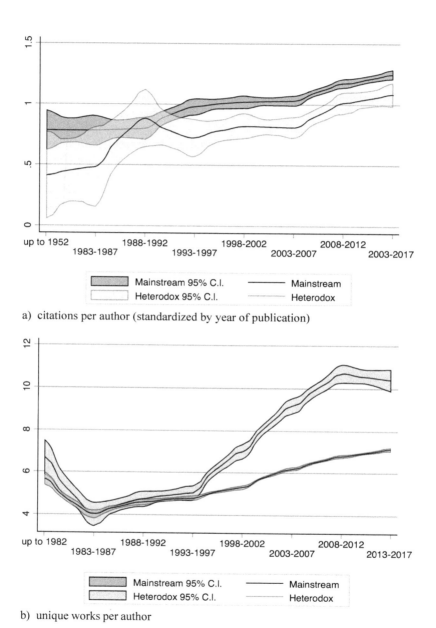

a) citations per author (standardized by year of publication)

b) unique works per author

*Figure 3.2* Visibility and productivity of heterodox and mainstream economists

loosen the relation between accrued citations and the quality of a publication: that is, increasingly, citations will reflect institutional characteristics and incentives rather than perceived quality.[12] More worrying, instead, is the impact that research evaluation seems to have on productivity. Further increases in the number of publications per author would have negative consequences for the discipline beyond the narrow scope of research evaluation purposes.

As noted in Chapter 2, every year, many more papers are published than anybody could read even in a decade. This produces what we may call a *paradox of abundance*: the larger the economics debate grows, the less democratic it becomes. Overabundance of publications makes mechanisms of selection and prioritization of what to read ever more important. In the face of oversupply, mainstream economists and especially those at the top of the economics food chain are right in arguing that they cannot be expected to read all the research done "at the bottom" – possibly, not even all that done at the top.

The solution to this problem will have to pass through both increasing the pluralism of the intermediaries that select and prioritize research (i.e. academic journal rankings, indexing and abstracting services, working paper series, and dissemination websites), as well as reducing the supply of papers. The two changes will have to take place simultaneously, because it is likely that if heterodox economists were unable to compensate for their lower average citations with more publications, their ratings within research evaluation schemes would be even worse. So focusing only on reducing the supply of papers – which per se is a necessary goal – could decrease the already low pluralism within the discipline. As much as the paradox of abundance is real and binding, democratizing the mechanisms of research selection and prioritization (journals, their rankings, etc.) seems to be the most urgent goal.

## Conclusions: economics at a crossroads

All sciences have low *input legitimacy*, as argued in the first chapter: the recruitment of new members of the profession largely has to be done by scientists themselves, with a risk of being self-referential. But in economics, the internal hierarchy and the degree of coordination of the graduate job market are such that legitimacy is lower than elsewhere.

The *output legitimacy* of mainstream economics has increasingly become a political issue for society at large. Long-term problems such as soaring inequality and job precarity or the ecological crisis compound with more recent events, such as the global financial crisis and the ensuing secular stagnation. The economics debate is certainly not the only, probably not even the main, cause of these social illnesses. But there is growing demand, among students as well as policymakers, for a different sort of economics that could accommodate and provide a rationale for more radical changes than current mainstream economics can.

The *throughput legitimacy* of economics, too, leaves much to improve: an excess supply of scientific papers reflects an environment in which everybody writes and nobody reads. In this context, research evaluation practices in which quality standards are mistaken for adherence to a specific scientific paradigm only make things worse.

All these trends are producing a visible crisis of economics. In response, some mainstream heavyweights argue for experimentation and greater liberality in starting a dialogue with heterodox colleagues,[13] while others have hardened their stance by either claiming that dissenters are deniers[14] or trying to get rid of all theoretical discussion assuming that empirics could be theory free and value free.[15] Heterodox economists, in turn, increasingly focus on interacting among themselves and developing a separate and autonomous paradigm, without the need to start each investigation from criticizing the mainstream.

A possible outcome of this growing divergence is that, as for example in France, heterodox economists may be tempted (or pushed) to part with mainstream economics and develop a new, separate discipline (Chavance and Labrousse, 2018). Such an outcome would not be unprecedented in the history of science or of the social sciences in particular. Without being the only cause, the *Methodenstreit* between Austrian economists and the German Historical School has certainly contributed to the development of sociology and of economic history as autonomous disciplines, separate from economics, little more than a century ago. This time, too, the separation would be driven as much by specialization by topic and field of study as by lack of communication among scholars of different methodological and theoretical traditions and by academic infighting.

These problems are common both to countries that have informal evaluation systems, such as Canada or the United States, and countries that have created formal schemes of research evaluation. But it is not by chance that the discussion became overheated in France, around the issue of formalized research evaluation. Preliminary international evidence suggests that systems based on formal rules reduce the scope for diversity, though more time is needed to finally establish an empirically observable causal mechanism. What can be said is that these systems by design exert a uniform pressure on individuals and institutions, which changes their constraints and incentives in a same way across the board. In other words, they produce a systematic impact.

Crucially, this impact can never be neutral in terms of contents and methods: research evaluation is bound to influence the development of science, partly in unexpected ways.

A relevant example is the geographical focus of economic analysis. Pasinetti (2006) highlights that top economics journals are US based (or at most UK based), as are their editors. They therefore tend to favor the study of the US economy, which is a legitimate editorial policy from several other points of view (it is the largest economy, it has been the ideational center of mainstream economics for several decades, etc.). However, if then within their evaluation systems the other ("peripheral") countries set publishing in the top journals as a prime goal, they inadvertently discourage the study of their own economies.[16]

To give a sense of how strong this impact can be, for the top ranked journals in some peripheral economies,[17] Figure 3.3 reports the share of published articles that contain a reference to the respective country (or population) in the title or abstract compared to the share of articles that contain the same reference in the top-5 journals. Some journals obviously choose to focus on their country's economy, publishing on this topic between one-third and half of their articles. Even the others, however, all publish many times more articles on their economy than the top-5 journals do. For the countries concerned, research published in these local flagship journals could be more relevant than that contained in a random article published in a top-5 journal – even if the top-5 journals all published articles of greater "quality"!

A first main implication of these reflections is asking if we really need systems of research evaluation whose criteria are centrally determined and uniform and that aim at comprehensively assessing the quality (or the "impact") of economics research across the board. Evidence suggests that we do not, at least for the sake of drafting competitive rankings, for the aim of allocating research funding, and probably even to select and promote research personnel. It thus remains unclear why so many countries introduced such schemes. One frequently mentioned possibility is the growth of an accounting culture and "new public management" methods of governance in the public sector. However, it would also be worth investigating the role within the political debate of economics research based on the linear model of science (assuming that basic research leads to applied research, which leads to product or process development) and on growth theories that mechanistically link research output to GDP growth.

Even if we did need comprehensive and formal research evaluation, it is doubtful that assessment schemes should be implemented so frequently and should require the evaluation of so many research outputs that, as we have seen, they further incentivize the supply of papers. If research evaluation must be an instrument of science policy, a central goal, at least in economics,

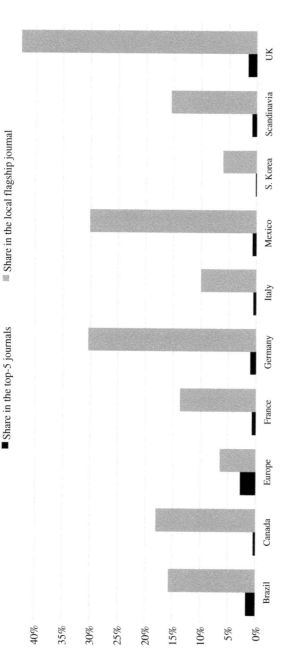

■ Share in the top-5 journals ■ Share in the local flagship journal

*Figure 3.3* Share of articles published in the top-5 journals and in flagship national or area journals since year 2000 that contain the country name or adjective in the metadata

*Notes:* country names have also been considered as adjectives; for Europe, "European Union," "EU," "E.U.," and "Europe" (as well as "European") have been considered; for Scandinavia and the Nordic countries: "Sweden," "Norway," "Denmark," "Finland," "Nordic," and "Scandinavia." The journals considered are, respectively: *Revista Brasileira de Economia* (Brazil), *Canadian Journal of Economics* (Canada), *Journal of the European Economic Association* (Europe), *Revue d'économie politique* (France), *German Economic Review* (Germany), *PSL Quarterly Review* (Italy; until 2007 known as *BNL Quarterly Review*), *Investigación Económica* (Mexico), *Korean Economic Review* (South Korea), *Scandinavian Journal of Economics* (Nordic countries), and *The Economic Journal* (United Kingdom).

should be to reduce the "salami slicing" of ideas into myriad small studies by evaluating a few pieces of research over long time intervals.

Second, if one wishes to set up large-scale systems of research evaluation, one cannot ignore that they affect the direction of economics research. Pretending that they do not only fosters conformism. If we wish to stay clear of dirigisme (which would be implied by the aim encouraging research in one particular domain or paradigm), the goal of such schemes should thus be to incentivize research in many *competing* fields and approaches simultaneously. That is, they should aim at fostering diversity and pluralism, increasing instead of decreasing the competition between research programs. This goal requires implementing at least three main principles:

1   aiming at neutrality in terms of research paradigms by standardizing peer review and bibliometric evaluations by the expected value of evaluations in each field and paradigm;
2   focusing on novelty and originality instead of quality or excellence: although all these concepts are elusive, the latter two are more value laden; and
3   allowing for the cultivation of different research profiles: in terms of research styles and methods; productivity and kinds of output; and especially in terms of professional trajectories, which must take individuals' backgrounds into consideration.[18]

These principles are ultimately inspired by the main goal of economics set out in the first chapter: feeding the democratic debate. Ultimately, what one thinks of the opportunity to have large-scale systems of systematic evaluation of research largely depends on what one thinks of the state of science and where one hopes to see it going (that is why so much space was devoted to this topic in Chapter 1).

In the case of economics, many policymakers and even more economists measure research outcomes by their recognition within the field, which they proxy by citation counts, which are then compared with aims of competitiveness and invidious rewarding of "excellence." The result is homologation and widespread follower behavior vis-à-vis privilege and power at the top. This seems to be the general trend in economics, only faster where formal research evaluation schemes are in place. Others care about pluralism and diversity of views and backgrounds and, as I have done here, argue that within economics there should be room for many different professional and intellectual trajectories. This is becoming increasingly difficult but arguably increasingly important in the face of obvious failures of current economics. Which side will prevail will determine what sort of, and how many, economics sciences we will have.

## Notes

1  For example, on the role of US financing of neoliberal collectives in Latin America, see the special issue of *PSL Quarterly Review* edited by Romero Sotelo (2019).

2  In December 2015, the Indian government set up a National Institutional Ranking Framework managed by the University Grants Commission (UGC). However, at the time of writing this work, the Parliament is discussing a bill that would reform the sector and replace the UGC with a new body.

3  The hint to "potentially up to two thirds" derives from knowledge of various cases (such as Tanzania, Vietnam, and other developing countries) where point-based or similar bibliometric systems are in place but for which full information on all data presented in Table 3.1 was not available. Some cases are more problematic to define, especially Germany's Habilitation system, which shares some features of a decentered research evaluation assessment and some of an academic title (a similar scheme exists in the German-speaking cantons of Switzerland). Even not counting such systems, however, German economists are still subject to a university-level formal research evaluation scheme.

4  For example, it has been shown that the *h*-index, widely used because it is less biased than simpler metrics such as the Journal Impact Factor, is not robust to trivial changes in the papers or citation counts on which it is based (Hicks and Melkers, 2012).

5  Already, J.S. Mill (and Alexis de Tocqueville before him) had convincingly argued that common opinion can come to control every detail of individuals' behavior and minds, even up to a point inaccessible to formal rules and institutions: "Society can and does execute its own mandates: . . . it practices a social tyranny more formidable than many kinds of political oppression, . . . it leaves fewer means to escape, penetrating much more deeply into the details of life, and enslaving the soul itself. Protection, therefore, against the tyranny of the magistrate is not enough: there needs protection also against the tyranny of the prevailing opinion and feeling" (Mill, 1859, p. 220).

6  One aspect is relevant to our discussion, though. It would appear that the so-called Goodhart's law ("when a measure becomes a target, it ceases to be a good measure") operates in this case, too, and citations may have lost their role as indicators of quality or scholarly impact – even assuming they originally had such a role. For example, Necker (2014) surveyed 426 economists, finding that 52% failed to read the content of works they cited, and 20% deliberately refrained from citing works published on low-ranked journals.

7  Empirically, there appears to be a positive but weak correlation between outcomes of research evaluation through bibliometric indicators and peer review in a recent Italian research evaluation exercise (Jappelli *et al.*, 2017). However, this finding is based on private information and is not replicable. At least in the case of economics, the result is not surprising, anyway, because the panel that de facto applied bibliometric methods of their choosing also selected the people who acted as reviewers, and therefore the correlation could be spurious and rather highlight the relevance of the referees' connections with the panel members.

8  By focusing on gender in this chapter, I do not mean to downplay other relevant dimensions of diversity of backgrounds. Unfortunately, about these dimensions, a smaller literature has developed so far. A recent survey by the American Economic Association among its members globally has found that economists feel

their profession has a lot to improve upon in terms of professional climate and environment (Allgood *et al.*, 2019). Only 34% of respondents feel "satisfied with the overall climate within the field of economics": 40% among males and 20% among females. Among people of color, the share is 34%, among people with disabilities 26%, and among LGBT people 26%. According to the survey, 48% of the interviewed women report having felt discriminated against or having been treated unfairly based on their sex, and the share among non-white economists is 29%. We need more, and more detailed, empirical evidence, but these first results are worrying enough.

9   Independently of their finding or not of gender-based discrimination, most studies report a lower number of submissions from women. For the case of economics, Hengel (2018) reports that female authors are held to higher standards within peer review and suggests that women may have internalized this trend, opting for a lower number of submissions of higher initial quality.

10  In unpublished work disseminated by the author on the internet; see ORCID: 0000–0001-5796–2727.

11  Data on the countries and the years of introduction of a formal research evaluation scheme are reported in Table 3.1. Citation and publication data are the same data from RePEc used in the previous chapter.

12  This impact has already been noted, for example, by Baccini *et al.* (2019), who have found evidence of strategic use of citations in the Italian scientific community (generalized across all disciplines), both in the form of strategic author self-citations and of citation clubs aimed at "gaming" the system.

13  For example: Akerlof (2020) concerning admissible research methods. More in general, on the lack of critical thinking in economics research, see, for example, Krugman (2009), Solow (2010), Romer (2016), or Rubinstein (2017). However, these criticisms have so far remained individual acts and have not produced a widespread debate on the usefulness and extent of pluralism in economics research.

14  See, for example, Cahuc and Zylberberg (2016), but also Jean Tirole's (2015) letter to the French minister of education, available in English translation at www.assoeconomiepolitique.org/wp-content/uploads/TIROLE_Letter.pdf

15  As implicit, for example, in Naidu *et al.* (2019).

16  In this respect, Alencar de Farias (2018) talks about research standards imposed by "WEIRD (Western, Educated, Industrialized, Rich and Democratic)" countries. See also Vessuri *et al.* (2014) and Bianco *et al.* (2016).

17  The journals were selected using the aggregate journal ranking produced by RePEc, selecting general interest economics journals that do not explicitly focus on the economy of a single country or area, such as *Japan and the World Economy* (58% of articles on Japan in the period), *The Economic Record* (57% on Australia), or the *South African Journal of Economics* (70% on African economies). The sample does not aim at representativeness but only at highlighting a general trend.

18  This has consequences in terms of the evaluation of individuals that must still be appropriately studied. For example, it is unclear whether anonymous peer review, in particular in the evaluation of individuals rather than publications, could lower or heighten gender-based discrimination.

# References

Aagaard, A., Kladakis, A. and Nielsen, M.W. (2019), "Concentration or Dispersal of Research Funding?", *Quantitative Science Studies*, DOI: 10.1162/qss_a_00002

Abramo, G., Cicero, T. and D'Angelo, C.A. (2015), "Should the Research Performance of Scientists Be Distinguished by Gender?", *Journal of Informetrics*, vol. 9, pp. 25–38.

Abramo, G., D'Angelo, C.A. and Rosati, F. (2014), "Relatives in the Same University Faculty: Nepotism or Merit?", *Scientometrics*, vol. 101, pp. 737–749.

Académie des Sciences, Leopoldina and Royal Society (2018), *Statement by Three National Academies on Good Practice in the Evaluation of Researchers and Research Programmes*, October 27, available at https://royalsociety.org/~/media/policy/Publications/2017/08-12-2017-royal-society-leopoldina-and-academie-des-sciences-call-for-more-support-for-research-evaluators.pdf

Adam (2019), "Science Funders Gamble on Grant Lotteries", *Nature*, November 20, available at www.nature.com/articles/d41586-019-03572-7

Adler, R., Ewing, J. and Taylor, P. (2008), *Citation Statistics: A Report from the International Mathematical Union (IMU) in Cooperation with the International Council of Industrial and Applied Mathematics (ICIAM) and the Institute of Mathematical Statistics (IMS)*, Joint IMU/ICIAM/IMS Committee on Quantitative Assessment of Research, available at www.mathunion.org/fileadmin/IMU/Report/CitationStatistics.pdf

Akerlof, G.A. (2019), "What They Were Thinking Then: The Consequences for Macroeconomics during the Past 60 Years", *Journal of Economic Perspectives*, vol. 33 (4), pp. 171–186.

Akerlof, G.A. (2020), "Sins of Omission and the Practice of Economics", *Journal of Economic Literature*, forthcoming, available at www.aeaweb.org/articles/pdf/doi/10.1257/jel.20191573

Alencar de Farias, S. (2018), "The Brazilian Little Way in Academia", *BAR: Brazilian Administration Review*, vol. 15 (1), DOI: 10.1590/1807-7692bar2018180035

Alesina, A. and Ardagna, S. (2010), "Large Changes in Fiscal Policy: Taxes versus Spending", in Brown, J.R. (ed.), *Tax Policy and the Economy*, Cambridge, MA: National Bureau of Economic Research.

Alesina, A., Giuliano, P. and Nunn, N. (2013), "On the Origins of Gender Roles: Women and the Plough", *Quarterly Journal of Economics*, vol. 128 (2), pp. 469–530.

Allesina, S. (2011), "Measuring Nepotism through Shared Last Names: The Case of Italian Academia", *PLOS ONE*, vol. 6 (8), e21160.

Allgood, S., Badgett, L., Bayer, A., Bertrand, M., Black, S.E., Bloom, N. and Cook, L.D. (2019), *AEA Professional Climate Survey: Final Report*, Committee on Equity, Diversity and Professional Conduct, American Economic Association, available at www.aeaweb.org/news/member-announcements-sept-26-2019

Amato, G. and Graziosi, A. (2012), *Grandi Illusioni*, Bologna: Il Mulino.

Angrist, J., Azoulay, P., Ellison, G., Hill, R. and Feng Lu, S. (2017), "Economic Research Evolves: Fields and Styles", *American Economic Review: Papers & Proceedings*, vol. 107 (5), pp. 293–297.

Appelbaum, B. (2019), "Blame Economists for the Mess We're In", *The New York Times*, August 24.

Baccini, A., Barabesi, L. and Cioni, M. (2014), "Crossing the Hurdle: The Determinants of Individual Scientific Performance", *Scientometrics*, vol. 101 (3), pp. 2035–2062.

Baccini, A., De Nicolao, G. and Petrovich, E. (2019), "Citation Gaming Induced by Bibliometric Evaluation: A Country-Level Comparative Analysis", *PLOS ONE*, DOI: 10.1371/journal.pone.0221212

Backhouse, R.E. and Cherrier, B. (2017), "The Age of the Applied Economist: The Transformation of Economics since the 1970s", *History of Political Economy*, vol. 49 (annual suppl.), DOI: 10.1215/00182702-4166239

Bagues, M., Sylos-Labini, M. and Zinovyeva, N. (2017), "Does the Gender Composition of Scientific Committees Matter?", *American Economic Review*, vol. 107 (4), pp. 1207–1238.

Baqaee, D.R. and Fahri, E. (2019), "JEEA-FBBVA Lecture 2018: The Microeconomic Foundations of Aggregate Production Foundations", *Journal of the European Economic Association*, vol. 17 (5), pp. 1337–1392.

Baumol, W.J. (2000), "What Marshall Didn't Know: On the Twentieth Century's Contributions to Economics", *The Quarterly Journal of Economics*, vol. 115 (1), pp. 1–44.

Baumol, W.J. and Bowen, W.G. (1966), *Performing Arts, the Economic Dilemma: A Study of Problems Common to Theater, Opera, Music, and Dance*, Cambridge, MA: The MIT Press.

Bayer, A. and Rouse, C.E. (2016), "Diversity in the Economics Profession: A New Attack on an Old Problem", *Journal of Economic Perspectives*, vol. 30 (4), pp. 221–242.

Becker, G.S. (1976), *The Economic Approach to Human Behavior*, Chicago: University of Chicago Press.

Berman, E.P. (2012), *Creating the Market University*, Princeton, NJ: Princeton University Press.

Bianco, M., Gras, N. and Sutz, J. (2016), "Academic Evaluation: Universal Instrument? Tool for Development?", *Minerva*, vol. 54 (4), pp. 399–421.

Blanchard, O. and Leigh, J.D. (2013), "Growth Forecast Errors and Fiscal Multipliers", *American Economic Review*, vol. 103 (3), pp. 117–120.

Bloch, H. (2010), "Research Evaluation Down Under: An Outsider's View from the Inside of the Australian Approach", *American Journal of Economics and Sociology*, vol. 69 (5), pp. 1530–1552.

Bol, T., de Vaan, M. and van de Rijt, A. (2018), "The Matthew Effect in Science Funding", *PNAS*, vol. 115 (19), pp. 4887–4890.

Bornmann, L., Rüdiger, M. and Daniel, H.-D. (2008), "How to Detect Indications of Potential Sources of Bias in Peer Review: A Generalized Latent Variable Modeling Approach Exemplified by a Gender Study", *Journal of Informetrics*, vol. 2, pp. 280–287.

Brooks, C., Fenton, E.M. and Walker, J.T. (2014), "Gender and the evaluation of research", *Research Policy*, 43, pp. 990–1001.

Brynjolfsson, E. (1993), "The Productivity Paradox of Information Technology", *Communications of the ACM*, vol. 36 (12), pp. 66–77.

Cahuc, P. and Zylberberg, A. (2016), *Le négationnisme économique et comment s'en débarrasser*, Paris: Flammarion.

Cardiff, C.F. and Klein, D.B. (2005), "Faculty Partisan Affiliations in All Disciplines: A Voter Registration Study", *Critical Review: A Journal of Politics and Society*, vol. 17 (3–4), pp. 237–255.

Cedrini, M. and Fontana, M. (2018), "Just Another Niche in the Wall? How Specialization Is Changing the Face of Mainstream Economics", *Cambridge Journal of Economics*, vol. 42, pp. 427–451.

Chavance, B. and Labrousse, A. (2018), "Institutions and 'Science': The Contest about Pluralism in Economics in France", *Review of Political Economy*, vol. 30 (2), pp. 190–209.

Cherrier, B. and Svorenčik, A. (2018), "The Quantitative Turn in the History of Economics: Promises, Perils and Challenges", *Journal of Economic Methodology*, DOI: 10.1080/1350178X.2018.1529217

Claveau, F. and Gingras, Y. (2016), "Macrodynamics of Economics: A Bibliometric History", *History of Political Economy*, vol. 48 (4), DOI: 10.1215/0018 2702-3687259

Coase, R.H. (1978), "Economics and Contiguous Disciplines", *The Journal of Legal Studies*, 7 (2), pp. 201–211.

Colander, D., Holt, R. and Rosser, J.B. Jr. (2004), "The Changing Face of Mainstream Economics", *Review of Political Economy*, vol. 16 (4), pp. 485–499.

Colussi, T. (2018), "Social Ties in Academia: A Friend is a Tresure", *The Review of Economics and Statistics*, 100 (1), pp. 45–50.

Comte, A. (1830), *Cours de Philosophie Positive*, Paris: Baillière.

Comte, A. (1851–1854), *Système de politique positive, ou traité de sociologie instituant la religion de l'Humanité*, 4 vols., Paris: Carilian-Goeury.

Corsi, M. (2007), "Thinking of Sylos Labini (or Sylos Labini's Thinking)", *Review of Political Economy*, vol. 19 (4), pp. 555–562.

Corsi, M. and D'Ippoliti, C. (2018), "The Democracy of Ideas: J. S. Mill, Liberalism and the Economic Debate", in Corsi, M., Kregel, J. and D'Ippoliti, C. (eds.), *Classical Economics Today: Essays in Honor of Alessandro Roncaglia*, London: Anthem Press.

Corsi, M., D'Ippoliti, C. and Lucidi, F. (2010), "Pluralism at Risk? Heterodox Economic Approaches and the Evaluation of Economic Research in Italy", *American Journal of Economics and Sociology*, vol. 69 (5), pp. 1495–1529.

Corsi, M., D'Ippoliti, C. and Lucidi, F. (2011), "On the Evaluation of Economic Research: The Case of Italy", *Economia Politica*, vol. 3, pp. 369–402.

Corsi, M., D'Ippoliti, C. and Zacchia, G. (2018), "A Case Study of Pluralism in Economics: The Heterodox Glass Ceiling in Italy", *Review of Political Economy*, DOI: 10.1080/09538259.2018.1423974

Corsi, M., D'Ippoliti, C. and Zacchia, G. (2019), "Diversity of Backgrounds and Ideas: The Case of Research Evaluation in Economics", *Research Policy*, vol. 48 (9), p. 103820.

Dasgupta, P. and David, P.A. (1994), "Toward a New Economics of Science", *Research Policy*, vol. 23, pp. 487–521.

Davis, J.B. (2006), "The Turn in Economics: Neoclassical Dominance to Mainstream Pluralism?", *Journal of Institutional Economics*, vol. 2 (1), pp. 1–20.

Davis, W.L., Figgins, B., Hedengren, D. and Klein, D.B. (2011), "Economics Professors' Favorite Economic Thinkers, Journals, and Blogs (along with Party and Policy Views)", *Econ Journal Watch*, vol. 8 (2), pp. 126–146.

De Benedictis, L. and Di Maio, M. (2016), "Schools of Thought and Economists' Opinions on Economic Policy", *Eastern Economic Journal*, vol. 42, pp. 464–482.

Deci, E. (1975), *Intrinsic Motivation*, New York: Plenum Press.

D'Ippoliti, C. (2018), "Many-Citedness", *INET Working Paper*, n. 57, available at www.ineteconomics.org/uploads/papers/WP_57-DIppoliti-revised.pdf

D'Ippoliti, C. and Roncaglia, A. (2015), "Heterodox Economics and the History of Economic Thought", in Jo, T.-H. and Todorova, Z. (eds.), *Advancing the Frontiers of Heterodox Economics: Essays in Honor of Frederic S. Lee*, London: Routledge.

Dobusch, L. and Kapeller, J. (2012), "A Guide to Paradigmatic Self-Marginalization: Lessons for Post-Keynesian Economists", *Review of Political Economy*, vol. 24 (3), pp. 469–487.

Dolfsma, W. and Negru, I. (2019), *The Ethical Formation of Economists*, London: Routledge.

Dow, S.C. (2004), "Structured Pluralism", *Journal of Economic Methodology*, vol. 11 (3), pp. 275–290.

Dow, S.C. (2017), "People Have Had Enough of Experts", *INET Blog*, available at www.ineteconomics.org/perspectives/blog/people-have-had-enough-of-experts

Dumont Oliveira, T. (2018), "From Modelmania to Datanomics: The Top Journals and the Quest for Formalization", *STOREPapers*, n. 2, available at www.storep.org/wp/wp-content/uploads/2019/02/WP-2-2018.pdf

Duvendack, M., Palmer-Jones, R. and Reed, W.R. (2017), "What Is Meant by 'Replication' and Why Does It Encounter Resistance in Economics?", *American Economic Review*, vol. 107 (5), pp. 46–51.

Eco, U. (1995), "Ur-Fascism", *The New York Review of Books*, June 22, available at www.nybooks.com/articles/1995/06/22/ur-fascism/

Ferber, M.A. and Brün, M. (2011), "The Gender Gap in Citations: Does It Persist?" *Feminist Economics*, 17 (1), pp. 151–58.

Fernández, R.G. and Suprinyak, C.E. (2016), "Manufacturing Pluralism in Brazilian Economics: The Role of ANPEC as Institutional Mediator and Stabilizer", *CEDEPLAR/UFMG Texto para Discussão*, n. 545, Belo Horizonte: Universidade Federal de Minas Gerais.

Fine, B. and Milonakis, D. (2009), *From Economics Imperialism to Freakonomics*, London: Routledge.

Forget, E. (1995), "American Women Economists, 1900–1940: Doctoral Dissertations and Research Specialization", in Dimand, M.A., Dimand, R. and Forget, E. (eds.), *Women of Value*, Cheltenham: Edward Elgar, pp. 25–38.

Fortin, J.-M. and Currie, D.J. (2013), "Big Science vs. Little Science: How Scientific Impact Scales with Funding", *PLOS ONE*, vol. 8 (6), e65263.

Foucault, M. (2004), *La Naissance de la biopolitique. Cours au Collège de France (1978–1979)*, Paris: Le Seuil.

Fourcade, M. (2015), "Economists' Ambivalent Authority", *New York Times*, February 9, available at www.nytimes.com/roomfordebate/2015/02/09/are-economists-overrated/economists-ambivalent-authority

Fourcade, M., Ollion, E. and Algan, Y. (2015), "The Superiority of Economists", *Journal of Economic Perspectives*, vol. 29 (1), pp. 89–114.

Frank, R.H., Gilovich, T. and Regan, D.T. (1993), "Does Studying Economics Inhibit Cooperation?", *Journal of Economic Perspectives*, vol. 7 (2), pp. 159–171.

Frey, B. (1997), *Not Just for the Money*, Cheltenham: Edward Elgar.

Gaffield, C., Corvol, P., Hacker, J., Parisi, G., Yamagiwa, J., Ramakrishnan, V. and McNutt, M. (2019), "Science and Trust", *Statement of the Science Academies*, Summit of the G7 Science Academies, March 25–26, available at www.academie-sciences.fr/pdf/rapport/Science_and_trust_G7_2019_EN.pdf

Gallup (2019), *Wellcome Global Monitor: First Wave Findings*, London: Wellcome Trust.

Gillies, D. (2014), "Selecting Applications for Funding: Why Random Choice Is Better Than Peer Review", *Roars Transactions (RT): A Journal on Research Policy & Evaluation*, vol. 2 (1), available at https://doi.org/10.13130/2282-5398/3834

Gordon, R.J. (2000), "Interpreting the 'One Big Wave' in U.S. Long-Term Productivity Growth", in van Ark, B., Kuipers, S. and Kuper, G. (eds.), *Productivity, Technology, and Economic Growth*, Boston: Kluwer Publishers.

Gordon, R.J. (2016), *The Rise and Fall of American Growth: The U.S. Standard of Living since the Civil War*, Princeton, NJ: Princeton University Press.

Gräbner, C. and Strunk, B. (2018), "Pluralism in Economics: Its Critiques and Their Lessons", *ICAE Working Paper*, n. 82, Linz: Institute for Comprehensive Analysis of the Economy.

Grimm, C., Puhringer, S. and Kapeller, J. (2018), "Paradigms and Policies: The State of Economics in the German-Speaking Countries", *ICAE Working Paper*, n. 77, Linz: Institute for Comprehensive Analysis of the Economy.

Gross, K. and Bergstrom, C.T. (2019), "Contest Models Highlight Inherent Inefficiencies of Scientific Funding Competitions", *PLoS Biology*, vol. 17 (1), e3000065.

Hamermesh, D.S. (2018), "Citations in Economics: Measurement, Uses, and Impacts", *Journal of Economic Literature*, vol. 56 (1), pp. 115–156.

Han, S.-K. (2003), "Tribal Regimes in Academia: A Comparative Analysis of Market Structure across Disciplines", *Social Networks*, 25 (3), pp. 251–80.

Hands, D.W. (2001), *Reflection without Rules: Economic Methodology and Contemporary Science Theory*, Cambridge: Cambridge University Press.

Hargreaves Heap, S. P. (2002). "Making British universities accountable: In the public interest?" in Mirowski, P. and Sent, E.-M. (eds.), *Science Bought and Sold: Essays in the Economics of Science* (pp. 287–411), Chicago, IL: University of Chicago Press.

Harley, S. and Lee, F.S. (1997), "Research Selectivity, Managerialism, and the Academic Labour Process: The Future of Nonmainstream Economics in U.K. Universities", *Human Relations*, vol. 50, pp. 1425–1460.

Heckman, J.J. and Moktan, S. (2018), "Publishing and Promotion in Economics: The Tyranny of the Top Five", *INET Working Paper*, n. 82, available at www. ineteconomics.org/research/research-papers/publishing-and-promotion-in-economics-the-tyranny-of-the-top-five

Heise, A. and Thieme, S. (2016), "The Short Rise and Long Fall of Heterodox Economics in Germany after the 1970s: Explorations in a Scientific Field of Power and Struggle", *Journal of Economic Issues*, vol. 50 (4), pp. 1105–1130.

Hengel, E. (2018), "Publishing while female: Are women held to higher standards? Evidence from peer review", *mimeo*, August 2018 revised version, available at http://www.erinhengel.com/research/publishing_female.pdf

Herndon, T., Ash, M. and Pollin, R. (2014), "Does High Public Debt Consistently Stifle Economic Growth? A Critique of Reinhard and Rogoff", *Cambridge Journal of Economics*, vol. 38 (2), pp. 257–279.

Heukelom, F. (2014), *Behavioral Economics: A History*, Cambridge: Cambridge University Press.

Hicks, D. and Melkers, J. (2012), "Bibliometrics as a Tool for Research Evaluation", in Link, A. and Vornatas, N. (eds.), *Handbook on the Theory and Practice of Program Evaluation*, Cheltenham: Edward Elgar.

Hicks, D., Wouters, M., Waltman, L., De Rijcke, S. and Rafols, I. (2015), "Bibliometrics: The Leiden Manifesto for Research Metrics", *Nature*, vol. 520, pp. 429–431.

Hirschman, D. and Berman, E.P. (2014), "Do Economists Make Policies? On the Political Effects of Economics", *Socio-Economic Review*, vol. 12, pp. 779–811.

Hodgson, G.M. (2011), "Sickonomics: Diagnoses and Remedies", *Review of Social Economy*, vol. 69 (3), pp. 357–376.

Hodgson, G.M. (2019), *Is There a Future for Heterodox Economics? Institutions, Ideology and a Scientific Community*, Cheltenham: Edward Elgar.

Horowitz, M. and Hughes, R. (2018), "Political Identity and Economists' Perceptions of Capitalist Crises", *Review of Radical Political Economics*, vol. 50 (1), pp. 173–193.

Jappelli, T., Nappi, C.A. and Torrini, R. (2017), "Gender Effects in Research Evaluation", *Research Policy*, vol. 46 (5), pp. 911–924.

Javdani, M. and Chang, H.J. (2019), "Who Said or What Said? Estimating Ideological Bias in Views among Economists", *MPRA Working Paper*, n. 91958, available at https://mpra.ub.uni-muenchen.de/91958/

Jayadev, A. and Konczal, M. (2010), "When Is Austerity Right?: In Boom, Not Bust", *Challenge*, vol. 53 (6), pp. 37–53.

Jo, T.-H. (2019), "Veblen's Evolutionary Methodology and Its Implications for Heterodox Economics in the Calculable Future", mimeo, presented at the *EAEPE 2019 Annual Conference*, Warsaw.

Jo, T.-H., Chester, L. and D'Ippoliti, C. (2018), "The State of the Art and Challenges for Heterodox Economics", in Jo, T.-H., Chester, L. and D'Ippoliti, C. (eds.), *Routledge Handbook of Heterodox Economics*, London: Routledge.

Kapeller, J. (2013), "'Model-Platonism' in Economics: On a Classical Epistemological Critique", *Journal of Institutional Economics*, vol. 9 (2), pp. 199–221.

Keynes, J.M. (1921), *A Treatise on Probability*, London: Macmillan.

Keynes, J.M. (1936), *The General Theory of Employment, Interest and Money*, London: Macmillan.

Klimina, A. (2018), "An Unfortunate Alignment of Heterodoxy, Nationalism, and Authoritarianism in Putin's Russia", *Journal of Economic Issues*, vol. 52 (2), pp. 517–526.

Knobloch-Westerwick, S., Glynn, C.J. and Huge, M. (2013), "The Matilda Effect in Science Communication: An Experiment on Gender Bias in Publication Quality Perceptions and Collaboration Interest", *Science Communication*, 35 (5), pp. 603–625.

Kregel, J. (1988), *Recollections of Eminent Economists*, vol. 1, Basingstoke: Macmillan.

Kregel, J. (1992), *Recollections of Eminent Economists*, vol. 2, Basingstoke: Macmillan.

Krugman, P. (2009), "How Did Economists Get It So Wrong?", *The New York Times Magazine*, September 2.

Kuhn, T.S. (1962), *The Structure of Scientific Revolutions*, Chicago: University of Chicago Press.

Lawson, T. (2003), *Reorienting Economics*, London: Routledge.

Lee, F.S. (2006), "The Research Assessment Exercise, the State and the Dominance of Mainstream Economics in British Universities", *Cambridge Journal of Economics*, vol. 31 (2), pp. 309–325.

Lee, F.S. (2009), *A History of Heterodox Economics: Challenging the Mainstream in the Twentieth Century*, New York: Routledge.

Lee, F.S., Pham, X. and Gu, G. (2013), "The UK Research Assessment Exercise and the Narrowing of UK Economics", *Cambridge Journal of Economics*, vol. 37 (4), pp. 693–717.

Lerback, J. and Hanson, B. (2017), "Journals invite too few women to referee", *Nature*, 541, pp. 455–457.

Lewis, W.A. (1954), "Economic Development with Unlimited Supplies of Labor", *The Manchester School*, vol. 22 (2), pp. 139–191.

López-Piñeiro, C. and Hicks, D. (2015), "Reception of Spanish Sociology by Domestic and Foreign Audiences Differs and Has Consequences for Evaluation", *Research Evaluation*, vol. 24 (1), pp. 78–89.

Ma, A., Mondragón, R.J. and Latora, V. (2015), "Anatomy of Funded Research in Science", *Proceedings of the National Academy of Sciences of the USA*, vol. 112, pp. 14760–14765.

Mäki, U. (1997), "The One World and the Many Theories", in Salanti, E. and Screpanti, E. (eds.), *Pluralism in Economics*, Cheltenham: Edward Elgar, pp. 37–47.

Mankiw, N.G. (2019), "Reflections of a Textbook Author", *mimeo*, March 6, available at https://scholar.harvard.edu/files/mankiw/files/reflections_of_a_textbook_author.pdf

Marcuzzo, M.C. (2019), "Note bibliografiche", *Moneta e Credito*, vol. 71 (284), pp. 391–395.

Marcuzzo, M.C. and Zacchia, G. (2010), "Peso alle citazioni o pesi alla numerosità? La valutazione degli economisti accademici italiani", *Politica Economica*, vol. 26 (3), pp. 409–440.

Marcuzzo, M.C. and Zacchia, G. (2016), "Is History of Economics What Historians of Economic Thought Do? A Quantitative Investigation", *History of Economic Ideas*, vol. 24 (3), pp. 29–46.

Marsh, H.W., Bornmann, L., Mutz, R., Daniel, H.-D. and O'Mara, A. (2009), "Gender Effects in the Peer Reviews of Grant Proposals: A Comprehensive Meta-Analysis Comparing Traditional and Multilevel Approaches", *Review of Educational Research*, vol. 79 (3), pp. 1290–1326.

Marsh, H.W., Jayasinghe, U.W. and Bond, N.W. (2011), "Gender Differences in Peer Reviews of Grant Applications: A Substantive-Methodological Synergy in Support of the Null Hypothesis Model", *Journal of Informetrics*, vol. 5, pp. 167–180.

Marx, K. and Engels, F. ([1848] 1969), "Manifesto of the Communist Party", *Marx/Engels Selected Works*, vol. 1, pp. 98–137, Moscow: Progress Publishers.

May, A.M., McGarvey, M.G. and Kucera, D. (2018), "Gender and European Economic Policy: A Survey of the Views of European Economists on Contemporary Economic Policy", *Kyklos*, vol. 71, pp. 162–183.

McCloskey, D. (2006), *The Bourgeois Virtues: Ethics for an Age of Commerce*, Chicago: Chicago University Press.

McCloskey, D. (2010), *Bourgeois Dignity: Why Economics Can't Explain the Modern World*, Chicago: Chicago University Press.

McCloskey, D. (2016), *Bourgeois Equality: How Ideas, Not Capital or Institutions, Enriched the World*, Chicago: Chicago University Press.

Mill, J.S. (1859), "On Liberty", in Robson, J.M. (ed.) (1969), *The Collective Works of John Stuart Mill*, vol. 18, Toronto: The University of Toronto Press.

Mill, J.S. (1865), "August Comte and Positivism", in Robson, J.M. (ed.) (1969), *The Collective Works of John Stuart Mill*, vol. 9, Toronto: The University of Toronto Press.

Mill, J.S. (1873), "Autobiography" (edited by Helen Taylor), in Robson, J.M. (ed.) (1969), *The Collective Works of John Stuart Mill*, vol. 10, Toronto: The University of Toronto Press.

Mirowski, P. (1992), *More Heat Than Light: Economics as Social Physics, Physics as Nature's Economics*, Cambridge: Cambridge University Press.

Mirowski, P. (2011), *Science-Mart: Privatizing American Science*, Cambridge, MA: Harvard University Press.

Mirowski, P. and Nik-Khah, E. (2017), *The Knowledge We Have Lost in Information: The History of Information in Modern Economics*, New York: Oxford University Press.

Mirowski, P. and Sent, E.M. (eds.) (2002), *Science Bought and Sold: Essays in the Economics of Science*, Chicago: Chicago University Press.

Moed, E.F. (2005), *Citation Analysis in Research Evaluation*, Dordrecht: Springer.

Mounk, Y. (2018), "What an Audacious Hoax Reveals about Academia", *The Atlantic*, October 5, available at www.theatlantic.com/ideas/archive/2018/10/new-sokal-hoax/572212/

Munz, P. (1993), *Philosophical Darwinism: On the Origin of Knowledge by Means of Natural Selection*, London: Routledge.

Murray, D., Siler, K., Lariviére, V., Chan, W.M., Collings, A.M., Raymond, J. and Sugimoto, C.R. (2018), "Gender and international diversity improves equity in peer review", *bioRxiv*, August 29, doi: https://doi.org/10.1101/400515

Naidu, S., Rodrik, D. and Zucman, G. (2019), "Economics after Neoliberalism", *Boston Review*, February 15, available at http://bostonreview.net/forum/suresh-naidu-dani-rodrik-gabriel-zucman-economics-after-neoliberalism

Necker, S. (2014), "Scientific Misconduct in Economics", *Research Policy*, vol. 43 (10), pp. 1747–1759.

Pasinetti, L.L. (2006), "A Note on Points of Dissent", in CIVR (ed.), *Relazione finale di Area, Panel: 13 – Scienze economiche e statistiche*, Rome: Comitato di Indirizzo per la Valutazione della Ricerca.

Pasinetti, L.L. and Roncaglia, A. (2006), "The Human Sciences in Italy: The Case of Political Economy", *Rivista italiana degli economisti*, vol. 11, pp. 461–499.

The Pew Research Center for the People & the Press (2009), *Public Praises Science: Scientists Fault Public, Media*, full report, Washington, DC, available at www.people-press.org/2009/07/09/public-praises-science-scientists-fault-public-media/

Phelps, E. (2013), *Mass Flourishing: How Grassroots Innovation Created Jobs, Challenge, and Change*, Princeton, NJ: Princeton University Press.

Posner, R.A. (1977), *Economic Analysis of Law*, Boston: Little, Brown.

Powdthavee, N., Riyanto, Y.E. and Knetsch, J.L. (2017), "Impact of Lower Rated Journals on Economists' Judgments of Publication Lists: Evidence from a Survey Experiment", *IZA Discussion Papers*, n. 10752.

Primack, R.B., Maron, M. and Campos-Arceiz, A. (2017), "Who are our reviewers and how do they review? The profile and work of Biological Conservation reviewers", *Biological Conservation*, 211 (A), pp. 177–182.

Rafols, I., Leydesdorff, L., O'Hare, A. and Nightingale, P. (2012), "How Journal Rankings Can Suppress Interdisciplinary Research: A Comparison between Innovation Studies and Business & Management", *Research Policy*, vol. 41 (7), pp. 1262–1282.

Reati, A. (2001), "Total Factor Productivity: A Misleading Concept", *PSL Quarterly Review*, vol. 54 (218), pp. 313–332.

Reinhart, C. and Rogoff, K. (2010), "Growth in a Time of Debt", *American Economic Review: Papers and Proceedings*, vol. 100 (2), pp. 573–578.

Rijcke, S.D., Wouters, P.F., Rushforth, A.D., Franssen, T.P. and Hammarfelt, B. (2016), "Evaluation Practices and Effects of Indicator Use: A Literature Review", *Research Evaluation*, vol. 25 (2), pp. 161–169.

Rocha, I.L. (2018), "Manufacturing as Driver of Economic Growth", *PSL Quarterly Review*, vol. 71 (285), pp. 103–138.

Rodrik, D. (2016), *Economics Rules*, New York: W.W. Norton.

Romer, P. (2016), "The Trouble with Macroeconomics", *mimeo*, New York: NYU Stern School of Business, September 14.

Romero Sotelo, M.E. (2019), "The Origins of Neoliberalism in Latin America: A Special Issue", *PSL Quarterly Review*, vol. 72 (289), pp. 85–90.

Roncaglia, A. (2005), *The Wealth of Ideas: A History of Economic Thought*, Cambridge: Cambridge University Press.

Roncaglia, A. (2011), *Why the Economists Got It Wrong: The Crisis and Its Cultural Roots*, London: Anthem Press.

Roncaglia, A. (2019), *The Age of Fragmentation*, Cambridge: Cambridge University Press.

Rubinstein, A. (2017), "Comments on Economic Models, Economics, and Economists: Remarks on Economics Rules by Dani Rodrik", *Journal of Economic Literature*, vol. 55 (1), pp. 162–172.

Sandström, U. and Van den Besselaar, P. (2018), "Funding, Evaluation, and the Performance of National Research Systems", *Journal of Informetrics*, vol. 12, pp. 365–384.

Sapienza, P. and Zingales, L. (2013), "Economic Experts vs. Average Americans", *American Economic Review*, vol. 103 (3), pp. 636–642.

Scharpf, F. (2003), "Problem-Solving Effectiveness and Democratic Accountability in the EU", *MPIfG Working Paper*, n. 03/1, available at www.mpifg.de

Schefold, B. (2018), *Die Bedeutung des ökonomischen Wissens für Wohlfahrt und wirtschaftliches Wachstum in der Geschichte*, Wiesbaden: Franz Steiner Verlag.

Schmidt, V.A. (2013), "Democracy and Legitimacy in the European Union Revisited: Input, Output and 'Throughput'", *Political Studies*, vol. 61, pp. 2–22.

Schumpeter, J.A. (1942), *Capitalism, Socialism, Democracy*, New York: Harper & Brothers.

Seabrooke, L., Ban, C., Helgadóttir, O., Nilsson, E.R. and Young, K. (2015), "Embedding GroupThink", presented at the *INET Conference*, OECD, Paris, April 8–11.

Shaikh, A.M. (2016), *Capitalism: Competition, Conflict, Crises*, New York: Oxford University Press.

Smaldino, P.E. and McElreath, R. (2016), "The Natural Selection of Bad Science", *Royal Society Open Science*, vol. 3, art. 160384.

Solow, R.M. (1956), "A Contribution to the Theory of Economic Growth", *Quarterly Journal of Economics*, vol. 70 (1), pp. 65–94.

Solow, R.M. (1987), "We'd Better Watch Out", *New York Times Book Review*, July 12, p. 36.

Solow, R.M. (2010), "Building a Science of Economics for the Real World", *Prepared Statement for Congressional Testimony before the House Committee on Science and Technology's Subcommittee on Investigations and Oversight*, Washington, DC, July 20.

Steinbaum, M. (2019), "Empiricism Alone Won't Save Us", *Boston Review*, February 28, available at http://bostonreview.net/forum/economics-after-neoliberalism/marshall-steinbaum-empiricism-alone-wont-save-us

Stephan, P. (2012), *How Economics Shapes Science*, Cambridge, MA: Harvard University Press.

Stockhammer, E., Dammerer, Q. and Kapur, S. (2017), "The Research Excellence Framework 2014, Journal Ratings and the Marginalization of Heterodox Economics", *mimeo*.

Sylos Labini, P. (1984), *The Forces of Economic Growth and Decline*, Cambridge, MA: The MIT Press.

Sylos Labini, P. ([2003] 2009), "Prospects for the World Economy", *PSL Quarterly Review*, vol. 62 (248–251), pp. 59–86. Originally published in *BNL Quarterly Review*, vol. 56 (226), pp. 179–206.

Tabellini, G. (2006), "Osservazioni sulla Nota di Dissenso di Luigi Pasinetti", in CIVR (ed.), *Relazione finale di Area, Panel: 13 – Scienze economiche e statistiche*, Rome: Comitato di Indirizzo per la Valutazione della Ricerca.

Tamblyn, R., Girard, N., Qian, C.J. and Hanley, J. (2018), "Assessment of Potential Bias in Research Grant Peer Review in Canada", *CMAJ*, April 23, vol. 190, pp. E489–E499.

Vessuri, H., Guédon, J.C. and Cetto, A.M. (2014), "Excellence or Quality? Impact of the Current Competition Regime on Science and Scientific Publishing in Latin America and Its Implications for Development", *Current Sociology*, vol. 62 (5), pp. 647–665.

Wang, J., Veugelers, R. and Stephan, P. (2017), "Bias against Novelty in Science: A Cautionary Tale for Users of Bibliometric Indicators", *Research Policy*, vol. 46 (8), pp. 1416–1436.

Weber, M. (1919 [2015]), "Politics as a Vocation", in Waters, T. and Waters, D. (eds.), *Rationalism and Modern Society*, New York: Palgrave MacMillan.

White, M.D. and Wang, P. (1997), "A Qualitative Study of Citing Behavior: Contributions, Criteria, and Metalevel Documentation Concerns", *The Library Quarterly*, vol. 67 (2), pp. 122–154.

Wicksteed, P.H. (1933), *The Common Sense of Political Economy*, revised and enlarged edition, edited by Lionel Robbins, London: George Routledge & Sons.

Williams, W.M. and Ceci, S.J. (2015), "National hiring experiments reveal 2:1 faculty preference for women on STEM tenure track", *PNAS*, 112 (17), pp. 5360–5365.

Wrenn, M. (2007), "What Is Heterodox Economics? Conversations with Historians of Economic Thought", *Forum for Social Economics*, vol. 36 (2), pp. 97–108.

Zacchia, G. (2017), "Diversity in Economics: A Gender Analysis of Italian Academic Production", *INET Working Paper*, n. 61, available at www.ineteconomics.org/uploads/papers/WP_61-Zacchia-Diversity-Final.pdf

Zaostrovtsev, A. (2005), "The Principal Conflict in Contemporary Russian Economic Thought: Traditional Approaches against Economics", *HWWA Discussion Paper*, n. 329, Hamburgh: Hamburgisches Welt-Wirtschafts-Archiv.

# Index

Page numbers in *italics* indicate a figure on the corresponding page. Page numbers in **bold** indicate a table on the corresponding page.